GOOD MORNING, CAPTAIN

50 Wonderful Years with Bob Keeshan

GOOD MORNING CAPTAIN

TV's Captain Kangaroo

by Bob Keeshan

Edited by Cathryn Long

Fairview Press • Minneapolis, Minnesota

Library of Congress Cataloging-in-Publication Data

Keeshan, Robert.
    Good morning, Captain : fifty wonderful years with Bob Keeshan, TV's Captain
by Bob Keeshan.
    p.   cm.
    ISBN 1-57749-000-2 (pbk.)
    1. Keeshan, Robert. 2. Television personalities—United States—Biography. 3.
Kangaroo (Television program). I. Title.
PN 1992.4.K44A3   1996
791.45'028'092—dc20
[B]

Cover design and page layout and composition by Glen-Michael DeCicco.

First Printing: October 1996
Printed in the United States of America

    00 99 98 97 96   7 6 5 4 3 2 1

Photo Credits

Unless listed below, all photos are courtesy CBS Television. Pages 4–5, 18, 9
Cowles Magazine, Inc./Library of Congress; 8 both, 9, 11–14, 16, 191, 194 both, 1
196–197, 204 both, 205 top—Keeshan Family; 15—© 1949, Robert E. (Bob) Smit
top—Frank Cannataro/ABC; 17 bottom—Whitestone Photo/ABC; 31, 32 top
bottom—Charles Neighbors, Inc.; 35 top left—THE LITTLE ENGINE THAT CO
mark of Platt & Munk, Publishers and is used by permission; 35 top right—Cov
OUS GEORGE by H. A. Rey. Copyright © 1941, renewed 1969 by H. A. Rey. Rep
mission of Houghton Mifflin Company. All rights reserved; 35 bottom left—MII
CATS written and illustrated by Wanda Gag, published by The Putnam & Gross
bottom right—Cover from MIKE MULLIGAN AND HIS STEAMSHOVEL by Vir
Burton. Copyright © 1939 by Virginia Lee Burton, © renewed 1967 by Virginia
Reprinted by permission of Houghton Mifflin Company. All rights reserved; 39
Press; 46—Sawyer's Inc., Portland, Oregon; 88, 89 bottom—Bronx Zoo; 89 top
Television; 94–95, 98–99—Manecke Family; 97 all—Emil S. Romano; 100–102
Leipzig, © 1957; 164 bottom, 165 bottom, 166—Jeffrey H. Finkle, Aries Photo
170—Al Day, WRDW-TV; 171 top, 183—Hart's Camera, Schottegatweg Oost
173 bottom—© 1996 Warner Bros. All rights reserved; 184–185—Reprinted w
Tribune Media Services; 186–187—Dartmouth College Archives; 190—Mark
Jack Brennan; 205 bottom—The Chicago Cubs; 207—Glen-Michael DeCicco

Publisher's Note: Fairview Press publishes books and other materials re
jects of family and social issues. Its publications, including *Good Morning,*
necessarily reflect the philosophy of Fairview Hospital and Healthcare Ser
ment programs.

The paper used in this publication meets the minimum requirements of
Standard for Information Sciences—Permanence of Paper for Printed Libr
Z329.48-1984.

This book is dedicated to my wife, A. Jeanne Laurie Keeshan, without whose advice and encouragement much of what is chronicled herein would not have occurred. Although I lost her this year after a prolonged illness, this is her life as much as it is mine, and for all of it I express my thanks and my love.

Contents

Foreword by Charles Osgood   1

Acknowledgments   3

Growing Up Happy   4

The Birth of a Show   20

Mr. Green Jeans   40

The Master Puppeteer   60

A Zoo Comes to You   84

The Stars that Shone   110

The People Who Made It Happen   134

Outside the Treasure House   160

Something to Laugh About   174

The Elder Statesman   186

Looking Back, Looking Forward   200

Captain Kangaroo Trivia   206

Foreword

Charles Osgood

Host of CBS "Sunday Morning"

Bob Keeshan has worn many different uniforms in his remarkable life. The uniform of a U.S. Marine. The academic robes of many an institution of higher learning, starting with my own alma mater, Fordham University. The uniform of a page at NBC. The costume of a clown named Clarabell on Buffalo Bob Smith's "Howdy Doody" show. And for more than three decades on CBS, the distinctive uniform of Captain Kangaroo. I'm willing to bet that most people who remember Clarabell—the mute, horn-tooting sidekick of Buffalo Bob—will not have realized until they read this book that the same young man also created the title character for network television's legendary and longest-running children's show, "Captain Kangaroo." Clarabell and Captain Kangaroo certainly did not look like one another. But think back. You never saw them in the same place, did you?

When Bob first put on the clothes of Captain Kangaroo, he was in his twenties, so young and slender that he had to wear a white wig and put padding in the costume so as to look more . . . substantial, shall we say. As the years went by, he would grow into the role of the gentle, avuncular character he had created. The real Bob Keeshan is a quiet, thoughtful man whose professional and personal life has revolved around children. He and his wife Jeanne raised three wonderful kids, who gave them six beautiful grandchildren. You have never met a prouder father or grandfather than Bob Keeshan.

As Captain Kangaroo, Bob could be a tough taskmaster on the set, though. A perfectionist, always demanding the best from his professional colleagues. But they understood he was always thinking of the kids out there. He never forgot all those little eyes and ears taking everything in, all those impressionable minds. He never talked down to children, never scolded or patronized them. Nor would he or any of the other adults on the show stoop to acting like idiots or getting a cheap laugh at someone else's expense. They were grown-ups. They were teachers. Bob understood that, and day after day, year after year, he not only amused and entertained children but also taught them, reassured, explained, told them stories, played with them, and stimulated their intelligence and their imaginations. He treated them always with kindness, love, and respect. And they responded in kind.

Today, wherever he goes, men and women old enough to have children and grandchildren of their own come up to Bob with great big smiles on their faces just to shake his hand and thank him for doing what he has done and for being what he has been. I believe this means more to Bob than all the honorary degrees (17), all the Emmy awards (6), the Peabodys (2), Gabriels (2), and other official honors that have been bestowed on him over the years.

Radio and television broadcasts disappear in an instant, literally at the speed of light. But on their way, for better or worse for a fleeting instant, they do touch millions of lives, one at a time. Thank you, Captain.

Acknowledgments

Cathryn Long has played a much broader role than editor of *Good Morning, Captain*, including researcher, coordinator, manager, negotiator, and critic. As a past viewer and a current editor, Cathryn's commitment to and enthusiasm for this project is greatly appreciated. Her hard work and dedication were very important and made this long overdue book possible.

Ruth Mary Manecke continues her support and involvement as the show's producer and manager. Her memory for so much of the show's rich history has made her an invaluable contributor to this book. Ruth is also, as always, a great team leader with the diplomacy and leadership skills that were key elements in the management of this book.

Jimmy Hirschfeld provided great detail on the team that he managed as executive producer and later as director of the show. Jimmy also has a great memory for people and anecdotes that preceded his tenure. For all his work and support over the many years, I thank him.

Ed Wedman, as publisher of Fairview Press, has shown enthusiasm for the project from the very beginning. His professional support and willingness in providing the resources of his organization have made this a viable and exciting project. Throughout this process, Ed has also become a good and valued friend.

Robyn Hansen, our editor at Fairview Press, was on the receiving end of a barrage of text, photos, and graphics. Her attention to detail and ability to juggle masterfully were critical to this book.

Laura Hunt Ramsey has also been an integral behind-the-scenes team member. Over the years, many of you received letters or photographs from this gracious lady after writing to the show. Her archival knowledge in tracking down photographs and information was helpful in producing this book.

Many CBS executives made it possible for the Captain to remain on television for more than thirty years. They know who they are, and they have my appreciation.

Last, but not least, I thank you, the reader, who as a child or a parent watched the program, laughed along, and made the Treasure House come alive. You helped me wake up Grandfather Clock, said "please" and "thank you," and observed "Be Good to Mother Day" . . . usually! Most importantly, thank you for caring for *your* children and having compassion for other people's children. That attitude bodes well for the nation's future.

Previous page
My youngest child, Maeve, once visited the studio, crawled into the Captain's lap, and carried on a lengthy conversation. I left the studio and changed into my street clothes. When I returned, Maeve ran to me and said with delight, "Daddy, Daddy, you should have been here! You just missed Captain Kangaroo!" It was precisely the reaction we wanted. The strength of her imagination reminded me of my own wonderful upbringing. This shot from the early years shows Mister Moose captivating my daughter Laurie.

Growing Up Happy

I always like to talk about the great potential in an infant, the potential for happiness and for accomplishment. We never know, when looking at a young child, what life that child will lead. There are so many influences, so many variables that determine the outcome of a life.

In retrospect, I could not have been a more fortunate human being.

I was lucky to have a loving set of parents and two older brothers, seven and ten, when I was born, who made my journey of discovery in this new world easy and pleasant. I was born in Lynbrook, Long Island, in June 1927, but I grew up in suburban Forest Hills, New York, where my family moved shortly after my birth. Those depression years were difficult for most American families. My dad, an immigrant from troubled Ireland twenty years before, was by this time an executive in a grocery company. This occupation eased the depression years for our family.

I hardly knew my dad when I was a child. Six days a week he was gone before the sun and I rose, and he returned home long after darkness fell. Daily, he traveled mile

Here I am as an infant in the arms of my maternal grandfather, James Conroy. My middle name, James, was for him.

A Sunday on the front bumper of Dad's Buick. This had to be a Sunday because every other day that Buick carried my dad on the many miles he traversed daily for his job.

upon mile in his trusty Buick, supervising stores of the Daniel Reeves grocery chain. The term "supermarket" was not yet in the lexicon. Each store was tiny, and there were hundreds of them in my dad's bailiwick. It was exhausting work, fourteen and fifteen hours a day, but Dad had a dream. He was one of those immigrants to the promised land where his family's future was worth any sacrifice. He saw his children through college and reveled in their accomplishments, accomplishments he knew would have been impossible a generation before in another place.

On Sundays, I would dog my dad's footsteps and adoringly leap to any challenge he presented. Gardening was his joy, and I remember, as a small child, being asked to pull a weed from between the flower rows. It was a tough weed, but I persisted, pulling and pulling until it yielded. I heard Dad's proud whisper to a neighbor, "Strong as an ox, that lad!" and my heart swelled with pride. Small praise will fire great accomplishment in a young child. No parent should forget that.

Young Bobby astride a horse in 1933 on a visit to the family farm in Ireland; my uncle Ned, who ran the farm; and my brother Jack.

In my dad's absence, my mother was the sunshine of my life. I adored her. Her soft, nurturing talents were known to all in our community, but especially to me. She was a loving woman and yet a mother who was demanding of me; she felt it was unfair to me to allow me to settle for less than I was able to accomplish. She provided an environment in which there was no doubt of her love, and that love was a warmth in my daily life.

They were wonderful, carefree days, and in retrospect, they prepared me for the work I have done in my lifetime. Imagination was encouraged in my family. Pretending was a daily part of our life. My sister Catherine was born three years after I was, and we, despite the huge gap three years can be to a young child, spent hours pretending. In the basement of our home we had a wind-up phonograph, not far removed from Thomas Edison. I can remember us playing Sousa marches and dressing in old parental clothes, coats and dresses dragging on the basement floor.

Some of my finest childhood memories are of soft summer evenings as dusk fell and before we were all called to our beds. We might be twelve or twenty in number, and we would play the games of childhood, physical games such as hide-and-go-seek or ring-a-lievo, and mental games that required brain power in search of answers. The cooperation required on those long summer evenings will always be with me, as will the friendships of childhood now so cherished. I am still able to summon up the fresh smells and visions of impending darkness of those summer evenings.

This enchanted life came to an end soon enough. My older brothers Bill and Jack left home for the navy and the army as the reality of cruelty in Europe and Asia encroached upon our golden world. New neighbors soon appeared in our community, refugees from the terror of the Nazis. The horrors, though not as horrific as what we were to learn of later, were impossible for so provincial a lad as I to grasp.

In a much more personal way, my world was shattered by the sudden death of my precious mother at the tender age of forty-five, when I was a fifteen-year-old. I don't think I ever fully recovered. From a good student I became a failure in a few short months. I cared about nothing. My brothers were away, my father was ill and mourning, and my young sister was affected even more than I.

We are often told how we can affect lives through our intervention. I was fortunate enough to have such an angel, a school guidance counselor named Gertrude Farley, who took charge of me and demanded that I find my way once again. Insistent she was, and it worked. It is a fabulous gift to be able to affect the life of another in a positive way. Miss Farley saved my life.

The war turned about and, after several years of desperation, the good guys were coming out on top. I knew I would be drafted in a few months in the summer of 1945, so I beat the draft board to the punch by joining the Marine Corps. The war in Europe had just ended when I reported for duty on Flag Day in 1945, two weeks before my eighteenth birthday. Anyone who has gone through boot camp in the Marine Corps will know what the next few months were like for me. Parris Island is not a place of fond memory, but it is a place of positive memories. I would never trade my Marine Corps experience for anything. The training, the character building, are second to none. To this day I call upon that training, and it has never failed me.

My younger sister Catherine and I in the mid-1930s. Catherine, to this day, with a far-away look, will often comment, "Bobby played with buttons," and it was true. Mother would give me buttons from her sewing box, and soon they became sailing ships navigating great oceans or herds of elephants serving royalty in India. Bringing my imagination to those buttons created kingdoms. What power there is in imagination!

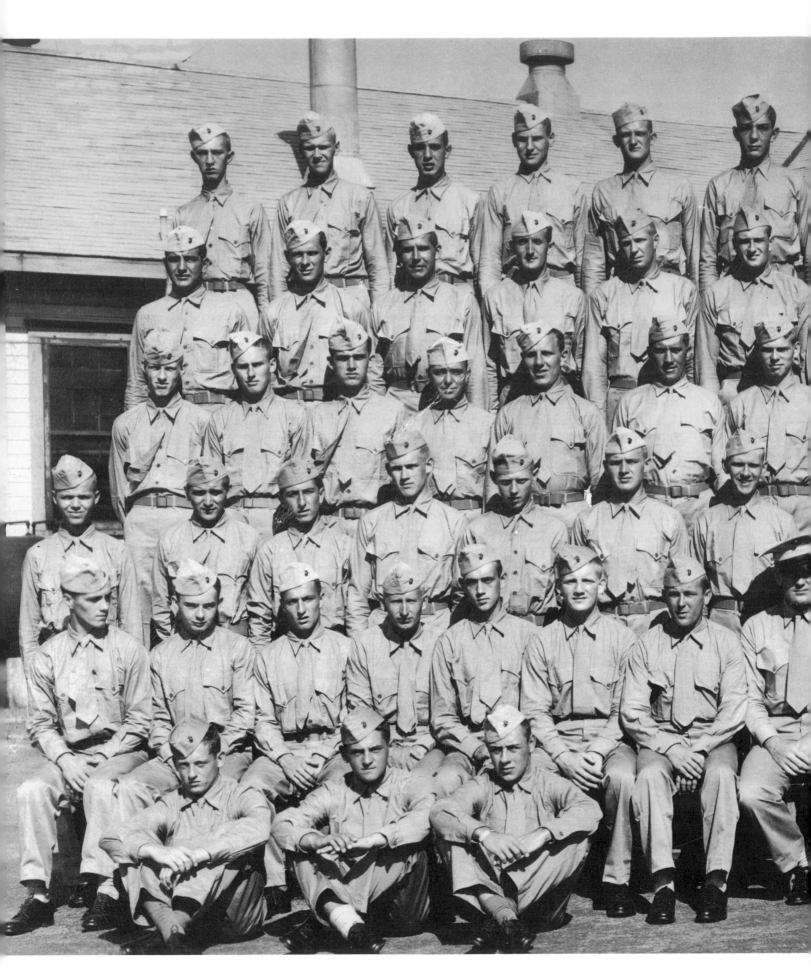

Previous page

I shall always remember Sergeant Hargrove and Corporal Taylor, my drill instructors who molded character in platoon number 345. Oh, boy! Did they mold character!

One of the first investments I made with my serviceman's discharge pay was in a sports jacket, and I took on the appearance of so many other young, pipe-smoking, college freshmen.

The marines were all training for the assault on the "home islands" of Japan, which we knew we would be part of in a few short months. The atomic age changed all that as my boot camp days wound down.

With the terrible war and all its painful experiences behind, the nation looked forward to a new era, and I was swept up in the euphoria along with millions of other returning servicemen and women. I had my three hundred dollars discharge pay and a promise from my uncle in Washington to help me through college.

I reclaimed an old job as a page at NBC Radio that had occupied me in my last year of high school, prior to the Marine Corps. I don't think NBC was too happy to have me back because there were so many college graduates of greater age ready to advance on the broadcasting career ladder. I recall a supervisor discouraging me from continuing in the job because he did not feel I had a future in broadcasting!

I hung in there, worked days, and went to college at night. I was not thinking of a career in radio at that time. I wanted to become an attorney and save the world. I like to tell audiences at speaking engagements that I intended to become a lawyer, not an actor, but years later, I'm not sure there's much difference between the two professions!

I liked working on the fourth floor of NBC Radio because it was quiet and I was able to hit the books while at my desk. Behind that desk was the fellow who ruled the morning radio time for WNBC in New York, a genial chap named Bob Smith. I did research for the daily feature "That Wonderful Year." Bob would play the piano and sing the songs from, say 1921, while the show's writer would weave a script talking about the cost of a loaf of bread, what it would take to put you in a Henry Ford-built auto, what you would pay for a snappy suit of clothes that year.

Television remained a future dream in 1946. A few television sets were around, but there were fewer than 100,000, and most were novelties mounted above the bottles of booze in saloons and barrooms. The parent company of NBC, RCA, was a manufacturer of television sets, and some executive figured that the best way to sell television sets was to provide television programs! What a stroke of genius.

Bob Smith had a children's radio show on Saturday mornings, and NBC asked him to bring his character from that show—an ugly rube named Howdy Doody—to host the new television program "Puppet Playhouse," starring the great puppeteer Frank Parris. The program went on the air on December 27, 1947. Bob had invited me to help with the production, but I missed that first show. It was the day of the "blizzard of 1947." I made the next broadcast a week later.

I helped with props and brought prizes to children who had correctly answered questions such as, "Who is buried in Grant's Tomb?" Wearing a sports jacket, I looked out of place, so the producer ordered me a clown suit and charged the makeup artist to create a makeup. My academic bearings served me well as I researched classic clowns. Soon a character named Clarabell was born, whose horn honked and who squirted Bob Smith and just about everyone else with seltzer.

Clarabell the Clown on "Howdy Doody" was created as a classic clown who never spoke. But I sure had fun honking the horn and squirting everyone with seltzer!

My wife, Jeanne Laurie Keeshan, about the time of our wedding. Jeanne was a very intelligent woman, a speech therapist and later a gerontologist, but most people remember Jeanne's sense of humor. She was a very, very funny lady, and she kept me smiling and laughing for forty-five years. Most of all, Jeanne was a spectacular mother, and I have three great children to prove it.

The act soon left "Puppet Playhouse" behind and became "Howdy Doody," starring Howdy's best friend Buffalo Bob, or to Howdy, "Mister Smeeth!" Howdy Doody and, months later, "Uncle Miltie" Berle brought television out of the barroom and into the living room. The most popular kid on any block was the one with the television set. Living rooms were packed each evening as American children cheered for Howdy Doody as he ran for president, leaving Tom Dewey and Harry Truman to the stuffy grown-ups. Motion picture theaters were empty on Tuesday evenings as Uncle Miltie, Little Boy Miltie, and other splendid characters took possession of show business. Not even free glassware and dishes could lure them back to the theaters on Tuesdays. Things would never be the same again.

Things were never the same for this happy clown after 1950, when a wonderful lady entered his life. Jeanne Laurie was a recent college graduate pursuing a career in the new medium of television. We met and were married six months later. The outside of the church was crowded with children and their parents looking for Clarabell and his bride. With me in mufti, they looked right past us.

I left "Howdy Doody" the last week of 1952. It had been a great experience, and what I know about the craft of live television (also applicable to tape) I learned from the master, Bob Smith. I was soon immersed in the business, doing local shows, the first of which was Corny the Clown and his dog Pudgy on "Time for Fun" at noon.

While still doing the noontime show, I was soon doing an additional character for a morning show. The character was Tinker and the program was "Tinker's Workshop." Tinker soon eclipsed the new "Today" show on NBC (in New York only because "Tinker" was a local show) and Jack Parr on CBS's morning show.

To play the grandfatherly character Tinker on "Tinker's Workshop," I grayed my hair and attached a mustache.

"Time for Fun" in the mid-1950s featured another friendly clown creation, Corny the Clown, and his dog Pudgy.

My children Michael, Laurie, and Maeve visited the set of "Captain Kangaroo." They met Bunny Rabbit, chatted with Mister Moose, and never realized the Captain was also "Daddy."

18

It didn't take long before "Tinker's" success prompted inquiries by CBS headquarters on Madison Avenue. A pilot "kinescope" was made, and in the autumn of 1955, "Captain Kangaroo" made his debut. In stentorian tones, the announcer said, "Boys and girls, CBS Television presents Captain Kangaroo and his Treasure House." The music started, the doors to the house opened, and an elderly man, jingling a ring of keys, made his way to a large desk and hung the keys on a nail.

Much of what happened after that day is chronicled in these pages. Few people, on that first day, realized that the elderly grandfather was but twenty-eight years old. I tell audiences, "I have grown into the part."

The Birth of a Show

The "Captain Kangaroo" show spanned almost forty years of television, almost ten thousand shows, from its initial broadcast on CBS Television on October 3, 1955, until its final airing on public television in August 1993. It is remembered by many generations of Americans; more than two hundred million people were touched by the program as child viewers, parents, or grandparents. The Captain is, for many, a fond memory of childhood, of simpler days, of a golden era. The reservoir of good and warm feelings held by these people for the Captain is tremendous.

Many people wonder how such a television program came about, how it got started. The Captain was the sum total of my television experience at that time, including different aspects of "Howdy Doody," "Time for Fun," and "Tinker's Workshop." As Tinker, I first explored the warm relationship between grandparent and child. Tinker's programming philosophy first brought us to the attention of CBS Television. Because Tinker was the direct predecessor, the father of the Captain, "Captain Kangaroo" was from the beginning a collegial effort. Many talented people helped create the program.

I have always believed that to educate, a teacher must engage the mind of the student, must be engaging or entertaining. We wanted to educate on the Captain, but our first priority was to entertain. We believed the "stuff" of entertainment was information and ideas that would benefit young people in growing up. The Treasure House was a place of fantasy and imagination. It had many toys and books, a place to make things, and a place to grow things, all presided over by a warm grandfather clothed in a jacket with large pockets. That's how the name came about, incidentally: the pockets similar to a kangaroo's pouch and the alliterative value of adding the rank of captain.

In the early years, the show usually began with me opening up the Treasure House accompanied by an upbeat tune and a big ring of jingly keys. Even this kind of consistency creates a sense of stability that children enjoy and find reassuring.

Mr. Green Jeans was originally conceived as the "Mr. Outside" to the Captain's "Mr. Inside." Hugh "Lumpy" Brannum took that role and made it his own. Yes, producers and writers had a hand in it: "He'll be a farmer"; "He'll show us animals"; "Let's dress him in green jeans and name him Mr. Green Jeans." But Lumpy created the character because he played himself, with all his caring and warmth that children at home sensed immediately.

A typically serene shot of Mr. Green Jeans, who shared his musical talents, knowledge of gardening, and respect for animals and nature with us every day.

From the show's beginning, Gus Allegretti created many of our other characters. Bunny Rabbit never spoke, but we always knew what he was saying anyway, and he almost always ended up with a carrot, or two, or three, in his hands. Grandfather Clock slept the show away (while Gus played other characters), until children called to him, when he awoke with a poem on his lips—which invariably led to further slumber. Gus's personality shone through Mister Moose as we all giggled at the ping-pong balls dropping on the Captain.

This very early photo depicts a Bunny Rabbit without his red spectacles. Added as an accessory soon after the show began, they soon became his signature. If you look carefully, you can also see Gus's arm behind the window!

A very young picture of me, Gus, and Mister Moose's cousin, Baby, during the early years of the show.

Although Grandfather Clock spent more time sleeping than awake, waking him meant we'd be treated to one of his sweet poems before he fell asleep again.

Early in the show, we had recorded a song about a dancing bear and held a production meeting to determine what to do with it. "How about Gus in a bear suit?" Gus shrugged his consent, and character was born. Not a word did that bear speak, but Gus's great artistry made him say all we needed to hear.

Dancing Bear dressed in sailor garb during the summer of 1959 when we filmed some spots aboard the S.S. Treasure House. Once introduced as a genuine character, Dancing Bear stayed the same throughout the years, the same gentle, soft-shoe shuffling, lovable, oversized bear.

Although the Town Clown required me to spend quite a bit of time in makeup, I truly enjoyed playing him. His classic clown character humorously displayed some of the frustrations that we experience on a daily basis.

I loved playing clowns—Clarabell on "Howdy Doody," Corny on "Time for Fun"—and when the technology of tape made it possible for me to tape inserts, we designed the Town Clown, with his baggy pants, big shoes, red nose, and enormous charm. He lived in a wagon on the edge of town, forgotten by a departing circus long ago. We all laughed at his inept attempt to solve the problems of ordinary life and then admired his innovative solutions.

Encouraging imagination was an important part of the show from the very beginning. The Treasure House hat tree let us use our imaginations by acting out different jobs and their responsibilities. Mr. Green Jeans was always a willing partner in playing at the hat tree. Here I also introduce children at home to various types of horns during a musical spot.

The Playtime Shoe Box contained construction paper, paste, and those round-edged scissors to make a world of fun things for mother or for holiday decorations. Music was always an integral part of the program, and we featured all kinds of music, from children's performers to classical favorites—and even an occasional performance by a newcomer to the musical scene, a chap named Elvis. Imagining what to be when we grew up was a common activity, and the hat tree provided men and women alike with the opportunity to try on different hats: police officer, baker, safari guide.

In those earliest days, very little programming was available on network television. The Captain was opposite the new "Today" show on NBC with Dave Garroway and a chimp named J. Fred Muggs. ABC's "Good Morning America" was twenty years away,

29

and most local stations featured cartoons from another era. But "Captain Kangaroo" was different from most programs because it was *television*, not derivative movie or radio programming like much of what was on the air. We were aware of the intimacy of television in the home, and we encouraged interaction with the child. On "Howdy Doody," I used to look at a monitor and see the televised Peanut Gallery laughing at Clarabell's antics. How did the children at home feel watching the Peanut Gallery and not seeing what they were laughing about? I believed that television was too intimate to allow a studio audience to interrupt my relationship with the child at home. Instead, the Captain would ask a question and wait to hear the response.

Everyone involved with the show believed that our audience was composed of intelligent human beings worthy of our respect and with potentially good taste. The show was not a lesson but entertainment of the highest quality. The finest teacher is

The early years on "Captain Kangaroo" were fun and exciting times for all of us. Television was a new and exhilarating medium, and we felt like we had all kinds of opportunities ahead of us. We made the Treasure House a magical place where anything seemed possible and safe.

an entertainer. Some teachers find that a demeaning concept, but to teach is to pass on knowledge, and being a scholar is not enough. A teacher must engage the mind of the student for knowledge to pass from one to another. If that is best done with a tap dance or a funny hat, so be it.

Our "education through entertainment" philosophy remained consistent for almost forty years, but the television medium changed dramatically during that time. In 1955, most television was broadcast over the airwaves and reception was sometimes iffy. Because production was live, production values were different than today, and we experienced many goofs. And goofs were *not* welcome on a program dealing with fantasy! A stagehand passing in front of the lens did not contribute to make-believe. The big rock candy mountain falling over on air shattered fantasy.

We were live on the CBS network every morning, and many people are surprised to learn that we actually did eleven shows a week. We started the first show at 8:00 A.M. Eastern time and finished at 8:59:20. In forty seconds, we reset the studio, props, cameras, actors, the works, and went on the air, once again, at 8:00 A.M. Central time.

Videotape arrived in 1956, but the limited number of tape machines were preempted by CBS News. It wasn't until 1959 that enough machines were available for us to tape the first show and play it back for the Midwest, eliminating our repeat show. Through all those first few years of the program, California and the West Coast aired the program a week late or later. California children saw Christmas Day on January 1, New Year's on January 8, and the nation's birthday on July 11. Do you suppose a week's delay of programming afforded an explanation for the California culture?

We created this cartoon specifically for our viewers with the expert help of TerryToons. The duo of Tom Terrific and Mighty Manfred the Wonder Dog went on wonderful adventures. Even the arch villains of Crabby Appleton, Pittsburgh the Pirate, and Isotope Feiny couldn't succeed against this terrific twosome!

To help fill the one-hour program, CBS had agreed to furnish "Captain Kangaroo" with twenty minutes of animation daily, which they intended to supply through their newly purchased TerryToons library and company. When viewing these cartoons, however, we found they displayed violence and cultural attitudes that, while acceptable to theatrical audiences of another era, were unsuitable, in our opinion, for our audience of young people.

CBS was very understanding and agreed to allow us to produce entirely new animation at TerryToons. One of our writers, Gene Wood, supervised the creation of a wondrous chap named "Tom Terrific." Tom gave us a sparkling four-minute adventure every day and filled our creative needs. Tom and his constant companion, Mighty Manfred the Wonder Dog, faced villain after dastardly villain, but by Friday morning all had ended well. A few years later, a baseball writer dubbed Mets pitcher Tom Seaver "Tom Terrific," and we took it as a compliment (though every time our Tom tossed a pitch to home plate, Mighty Manfred charged, thinking he saw a meatball instead. Manfred loved his dinner!).

Gene Wood's team also created "Lariat Sam," who rode his trusty steed Tippy Toes into many a sunset. After these two, we purchased animation that was gentle and appropriate for our audience, such as "Crystal Tipps and Alistair" and "The Toothbrush Family." Another hugely popular feature was our interactive *Picturepages*, produced with our friend Bill Cosby. Many animated spots came from British television, which shared our philosophy about protecting young audiences.

Lariat Sam and his faithful steed Tippy Toes were also popular custom-made cartoon characters. Whatever adventure they got tangled up in, they always seemed to end up riding off into the sunset as heroes.

"Crystal Tipps and Alistair" was a charming, soft, and gentle cartoon series. We looked far and wide before purchasing this series from the British, a culture that puts great emphasis on gently nurturing their children.

Although it wasn't animation, the Magic Drawing Board added much of the same feeling to the show, with the addition of music we chose to accompany it. Gus Allegretti and director Peter Birch made this feature entertaining, informative, and very popular.

It was difficult to pull off. Gus was a great artist as well as puppeteer. Magic Drawing Board was a shadow box faced with a plastic sheet. Gus would dress in black, including a hood with eye-slits, and from inside the shadow box would draw with a black-taped flow pen. The slightest ray of light destroyed the effect. Gus would "animate," or draw to songs such as "The Big Rock Candy Mountain" or "Puff the Magic Dragon." Gus also had to draw *backwards* because he was facing the camera. The most difficult time came when he had to draw numbers or letters of the alphabet backwards!

Picturepages was a colorful, interactive newsletter that we used as a fun learning tool. Thanks to the help of Bill Cosby, it became amazingly popular on the show by the 1980s. Children at home could either work along with us from their television sets or send postcards requesting *Picturepages* to work on at home. As you can see, we received thousands of requests for *Picturepages*.

One of the most popular features of "Captain Kangaroo" from the very beginning was the daily segment we called "Reading Stories." Each day we would take a book from our library of children's literature, and the Captain would read while cameras focused on the illustrations.

From the very beginning, "Reading Stories" was an important time on the show each day. We felt it was important to share different types of reading materials, including newspapers, funny pages, books, and encyclopedias.

We read more than 5,000 books on the show, many of them multiple times. We know the most popular stories were *Mike Mulligan and His Steam Shovel* (Remember Mary Ann? What happened to her when the town hall basement digging was complete?) and *Make Way for Ducklings* (Who can forget Officer Clancy stopping Boston traffic for those ducklings? What were their names again?). In *Stone Soup* we learned about generosity; in *Caps for Sale* we found out what the expression "monkey see, monkey do" means. *The Little Engine That Could* was always inspirational to me. Remember *Andy and the Lion, Millions of Cats, The Little Red Lighthouse, My Mom Travels a Lot, Gwendolyn the Miracle Hen, Even If I Did Something Awful, Sometimes Mama and Papa Fight, A Bug of Some Importance, Corduroy, The Story about Ping, Grandfather and I, A Book of Hugs*, and hundreds, no, thousands more. So many of these books are still around. What a gift a parent presents to a child with a good "reading story."

In *Books to Grow By,* my recent guide to children's literature, I talk about many of the great parent-child relationships built while reading. I am a believer in reading to children when they first come home from the hospital. No, they will not understand the words, but they will perceive the parent's voice and likeness in a unique way. Reading to a child forms a great bond that can last a lifetime.

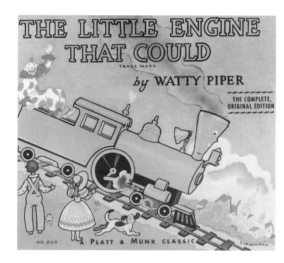

Books to Grow By also talks about the giving of values from parent to child. I review books by age appropriateness and by virtue, virtues such as generosity, truth, or self-discipline. I give parents a nifty idea of what to do when a child asks for a story the umpteenth time. "Goofy storytelling" is a strategy straight from "Captain Kangaroo" and will make any parent a top-of-the-line entertainer, a delight to children.

We often took the time to sit down to read. Occasionally the rest of the Treasure House family would share in the experience.

To this day people tell me and write to me saying how influenced they were by the books read on the show—some saying that they have become teachers or professors as a result.

We recognized the importance of being sensitive to the changing multicultural environment. Here Mister Moose looks on and listens as we read a basic Spanish book.

Even on location, as we are here in Popcorn Village in Nashville, Tennessee, we took precious time for "Reading Stories."

Apparently, I even have storytelling talents with animals as I read to my orangutan friend at Busch Gardens in Florida. He actually pointed to the pictures as I read to him!

Our nation is shared by diverse cultures, and we attempted in reading stories and other ways to make children sensitive to these many cultures. At one point, we asked my good friend and Dartmouth linguistics professor John Rassias to help us develop a program that would offer some Spanish language and Hispanic culture by using our show characters in many situations. In no time, Mister Moose learned to use Spanish to drop ping-pong balls on you-know-who! *Si!*

Books are such an integral part of any culture, such a treasure to give to children. There is talk abroad these days that the computer will alter the importance of books. I do not agree. The computer, the compact disc, and video games are all based on the written word. Johannes Gutenberg would hardly have conceived of the changes in how the written word is recorded and read, but after all these years, it is still the written word, and its joys distinguish humankind from other creatures of the earth. I believe the Captain contributed to that joy. As Henry Adams said, "A teacher affects eternity; he can never tell where his influence stops." I hope the Captain has been a good teacher.

Marlo Thomas introduced our audience to many of her fine ideas in her book *Free to Be You and Me.* Our dear guest Margaret Hamilton (the Wicked Witch of the West from *The Wizard of Oz*) shared "Reading Stories" time with our young viewers.

A contemporary shot of me as Bob Keeshan, the author, sharing fun ideas from my *Family Fun Activity Book* with some of my young friends.

Books to Grow By is a wonderful guide for parents to choose books and reinforce values with their children from birth to age eight. It is largely a compilation of favorite books read over many years on the show.

Previous page
Mr. Green Jeans was fondly remembered for many of his activities on the show—such as his gardening, singing, and guitar playing—but he is best remembered for the many animals he shared with us every day of the show. This shot is from the early days and shows Lumpy holding a beautiful African gray goose.

Mr. Green Jeans

Surely one of the most popular characters on "Captain Kangaroo" was Mr. Green Jeans, played by Hugh (Lumpy) Brannum. Lumpy would never reveal the origin of his nickname; he implied that it originated in adolescence and would comment no further.

Lumpy's background was not in acting but in music. He was born in rural Sandwich, Illinois. His father was a minister of the gospel and, to hear Lumpy tell it, was a stern taskmaster. Music interested Lumpy from an early age. He played some brass instruments, such as the tuba and trombone, but his talent was for the bass violin. He also played a pretty sweet guitar, and on the rare occasion when he plucked the banjo, feet would stomp across the nation.

Lumpy left Illinois to spend his college years at Redlands in faraway California. That was in the twenties and thirties, and California had not grown into its present culture or population. The jazz bug took a bite of Lumpy, and he spent his post-college years strummin' the bass at a small California radio station and in bands at jazz spots up and down the west coast. Along came the Second World War, and somehow Lumpy ended up a marine! It has often been noted with surprise that two of the principal characters on a gentle children's show—Mr. Green Jeans and Captain Kangaroo—each served in the rugged Marine Corps. Lumpy and I shared that kinship, and we agreed that the training of the corps instilled a discipline that served each of us well in our profession.

Lumpy ended up playing in a marine band led by Bob Crosby, Bing's brother, who had brought together a group of very talented jazz musicians. In relaxed moments in our studio, Lumpy told many tales about the reluctance of these musicians to play at parade-ground ceremonies or at an officer's club dance. These cats wanted to play *their* music, which in no way resembled the stuff Glenn Miller and Guy Lombardo were playing for America.

The war ended, but the music played on. Lumpy and four friends formed their own group known as The Four Squires. The orchestra leader Fred Waring hired them, and after the group broke up, Lumpy stayed on plucking bass for Fred Waring and His Pennsylvanians. This was a *really* big band, many musicians, specialty groups, and the very famous glee club. Lumpy and his wife Peggy moved to Shawnee-on-the-

Lumpy's Mr. Green Jeans was created as the "Mr. Outdoors" to my "Mr. Indoors." He always made time to nurture the plants in the garden, teach us about animals and the environment, sing a song with us on his guitar, or greet a passerby as he rocked in his favorite chair. He was as important to the Treasure House as the Captain.

Delaware, which served as headquarters for this huge musical organization. It was at Shawnee that Lumpy first tended his vegetable garden. In later years, the cast and staff of "Captain Kangaroo" all dreaded Monday mornings, when Lumpy would appear after a weekend in Pennsylvania to grumble and groan about the worms who had burrowed into his tomatoes, the birds who had dive-bombed his corn, and the rabbits and deer who subsisted on his green leaves! It was hard to take at five o'clock in the morning. After all this venting, Lumpy felt better and informed us that these creatures had to eat, after all. He just wished they would sit down to someone else's table!

Fred Waring and His Pennsylvanians were very popular in radio, occupying an early-evening spot five days a week. As a page at NBC, I helped seat the audiences for

Mr. Green Jeans was always a willing partner of mine, whether it required helping me create dessert in the magical pie machine, manning the helm of the SS Treasure House (summer of 1959), or dressing up as Santa Claus at Christmas time.

Sharing interesting information about animals and their habitats was a very special part of Mr. Green Jeans's role at the Treasure House. It came naturally to him, regardless of whether the animal was an African gray parrot, a full-grown elephant, a lion cub, or a young orangutan. He was as genuinely caring and concerned about humanity, animals, and the environment as he appeared.

Good Morning, Captain   Mr. Green Jeans

The very talented Lumpy
Brannum loved playing
other characters,
including playing the
bass fiddle as the Old
Folksinger, a natural for
his musical talents;
dispensing great foolish-
ness as the Professor; or
looking pensive and
nautical as a sailor.

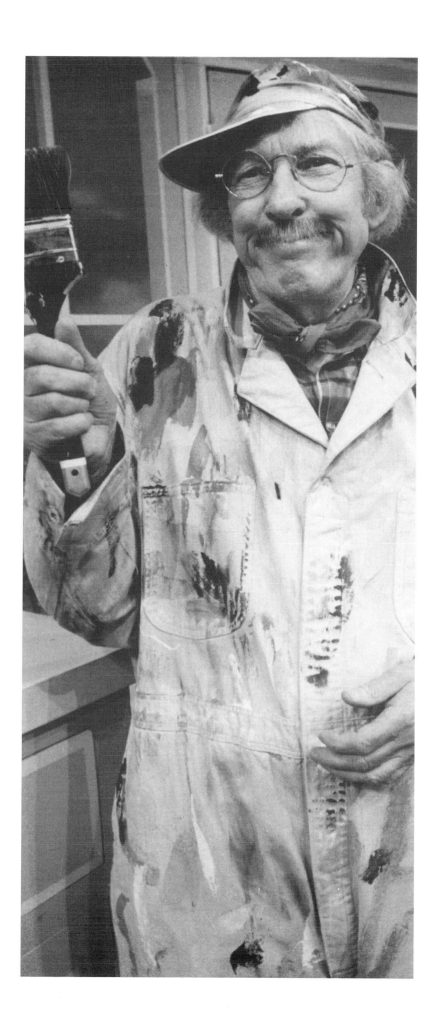

In addition to Mr. Green Jeans, Lumpy also enjoyed the ongoing characters of Percy and Mr. Bainter the Painter.

As with the Captain and the other Treasure House cast, Lumpy had fun participating as Mr. Green Jeans and as other characters when guest celebrities visited. Here's Lumpy with Andy Griffith as a western cowboy, with George Rose as an astronaut of sorts, with Hermione and Gingold as a king, with Mike Farrell and Lola Falana as an events judge.

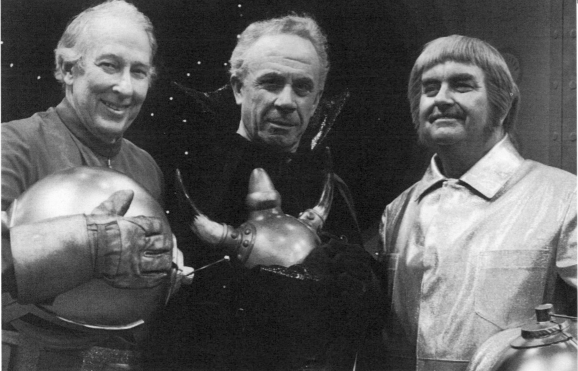

their radio broadcasts. Bass player Lumpy Brannum was featured with special material for young people, "Stories of Uncle Lumpy and Little Orly." These were short gems that Lumpy created and that were performed against musical background provided by, you guessed it, Lumpy Brannum.

In 1954, Lumpy did an afternoon television program on the local ABC station

54

WABC-TV called "Uncle Lumpy's Cabin," in which Lumpy played Lumpy, always himself, and Tom Howell played a friendly postman. They included many delightful tales
in these daily broadcasts, including Little Orly stories and such charmers as "Horace,
the Milk Wagon Horse." I was at the same station at the same time with my morning
show "Tinker's Workshop" and my noontime "Time for Fun." On the same station was

Ruth Manecke, who later supplied all the great animals for the "Captain," in her own show, "Animal Fun Time." WABC-TV eventually lost us all when we created "Captain Kangaroo."

During those ABC days, Jack Miller (my "Time for Fun" producer and my partner in the early "Captain" days) and I produced some records, and Lumpy worked as talent in a few of them. When it came time to produce "Captain Kangaroo," I asked

Lumpy if he would like to be "Mr. Outside" to my "Mr. Inside." He agreed—and a character was born. There were many decisions made by producers and writers—the new character would be a farmer, care for the many animals, wear green jeans, play some music—but it was Lumpy's character from the beginning because he played himself. His warmth, his love for children, and his concern for the earth were all part of his own personality.

Lumpy played scenes as various characters with some of our fun guest celebrities, such as Cyril Ritchard, Eli Wallach, and Dorothy Loudon.

Lumpy Brannum was a leader in the ecology movement back in the 1950s, long before "environment" became a buzzword in the American lexicon. He would tell our audience about the need to share our earth, protect our world, plan for the future. For these spots, there was little, if any, preparation given to Lumpy; it all came from his mind and his heart. He had a genuine love for the earth and all its creatures, great and small.

Lumpy's love for young people was not something he wore on his green sleeve. In the studio, he might read a newspaper report about some children being abused in faraway India, and the article would incite in him a quiet but righteous anger. He didn't know those children, but his love extended to all children.

Our relationship was close. He was not my *best* friend, nor I his. After a ten- or twelve-hour studio day, we went our own ways. But we had an enormous respect for each other, and certainly a great affection. In the early ad-lib days of the show, he usually knew where I was going long before I got there. I was pretty skilled at reading his mind, also. The success of most show business presentations comes from human chemistry, from the interaction of writers, producers, talent. Lumpy, Gus Allegretti, and I had that chemistry, and it endured through almost ten thousand broadcasts.

Opposite

Unfortunately, Lumpy is no longer with us, but his kindness and special warmth as Mr. Green Jeans are well remembered. Millions of children, parents, and grandparents were touched by his character throughout all the years on the show. His presence in all our lives is truly eternal.

The Master Puppeteer

An essential element in the successful chemistry of "Captain Kangaroo" was Cosmo Francis Allegretti, or, as he is known to the world, Gus. Gus Allegretti might be called a puppeteer, and he is a brilliant puppeteer, but it only begins to describe his talents. He is a very fine and versatile actor, the kind of imaginative performer who makes writers proud of their material. The range of characters he performed and the variety of material he handled routinely were nothing short of astounding. Working with Gus Allegretti is a creative joy.

Gus was, in the best and old-fashioned sense, a kid from Brooklyn, when people from that borough took great pride in their origins and in their particular culture, including the Brooklyn Dodgers and Ebbets Field. Gus's parents came to America from Calabria, and to say that Gus is Italian is to utter an understatement. He is also a fiercely proud man, and for good reason. He is very well educated and an awesome debater. I know because he verbally ran rings around me by setting many an unforeseen linguistic trap. He loves language; he is an etymologist at heart, fascinated by the history and origin of words.

An early recording we made featured a song about a dancing bear. "How do we perform this number?" asked the writers and producers. "How about Gus in a bear suit?" we answered. We got so much fan mail, he became a regular. Doing Dancing Bear was very challenging as the costume was large and became heavy and warm under the studio lights. Here is a rare shot of Gus putting up his paws between scenes.

ABC and television station WABC-TV gave us many talented people. Lumpy Brannum, producers Jack Miller and Bob Claver, zoologist Ruth Manecke, and I were all products of that place. Gus had been a puppeteer on "Rootie Kazootie," an early children's program seen on NBC and later on ABC. Bob Claver became friendly with Gus in those ABC days, and when we were putting the "Captain" show together, Bob recommended we talk to Gus.

One of the Treasure House's most lovable characters was Dancing Bear. Although huge in size, he was known for his soft-shoe routines and his gentle nature and happy-go-lucky attitude. Here Dancing Bear takes a spin on the SS Treasure House deck with me and Chuck McCann, gets a bear hug from actress Gwen Verdon as he gingerly holds a kitten, and giggles with Broadway actress Andrea McArdle of "Annie" fame.

Mister Moose and Bunny Rabbit, inseparable companions and partners in plotting against the Captain. Some psychologically inclined viewers might surmise that these two were surrogates for children, demonstrating their playful power over an adult.

We interviewed Gus in a room at the Warwick Hotel, which housed our temporary offices. I suppose the producer and I were pretty demanding in what we were looking for, and we asked some pointed questions. I liked Gus, but I remember inquiring if he really wanted to work on another children's show. At that time, Gus was working as

Bunny Rabbit was very expressive for a creature who didn't speak. Somehow he always bamboozled the Captain out of a bunch of carrots. Bunny Rabbit, a member of the Treasure House from the first day, actually began his career without his spectacles. Apparently he didn't eat enough carrots, though, because he soon donned his little red glasses, and they have been a distinguished and permanent part of his character ever since.

an illustrator for a retail company—a job he hated—but it was clear he was going to work on *his* terms or not at all.

Am I lucky we all got together. "Captain Kangaroo" would never have been the same without Gus Allegretti. Just look at the variety of characters he brought to life: Bunny Rabbit, Mister Moose, Dancing Bear, Rollo the Hippopotamus, Miss Worm (what a voice!), Grandfather Clock, Magic Drawing Board, Fred from Channel One, Cornelius the Walrus, Bernard the very large dog, Dennis the Apprentice, and many, many more. Gus did the live art and portrayals of songs (for example, "The Big Rock Candy Mountain," "Busy Hands Are Happy Hands," "Puff, the Magic Dragon," "The

Horse in Striped Pajamas," and hundreds more). He also played itinerant characters from kings to knaves to little old ladies. Gus's talent is unbounded.

Perhaps the greatest "Captain Kangaroo" memory for yesterday's children, today's adults, is of a Gus Allegretti creation—Mister Moose and the ping-pong balls. I am often asked what word or signal Mister Moose engaged to trigger the fall of those spheres. There were many cues, of course, ranging from knock-knock jokes to rhymes to riddles. I am grateful to Gus for this wonderful addition to the show, but I am able to write these words today because of a change made the first time we performed that ritual. The writer had called for golf balls to fall and I said, "No!"

Another favorite was the raspy-voiced Mister Moose. He often had a clever riddle or knock-knock joke that would inevitably end up with the naive Captain being barraged with ping-pong balls. Pulling a fast one on the ol' Captain was something that kids loved for more than thirty years. It never got old!

From the early days, we would ask children to help wake up the ever-sleeping Grandfather Clock. Remember how we used to do it? I would count to three, and children would call out from their TV sets at home "Grandfather!" Presto! Grandfather Clock (Gus) would awaken and reward us with a poem or a riddle, every one of which ended with him returning to his slumber.

Other puppet figures and characters that Gus created and/or played included the operatic singing Miss Worm; Rollo the Hippopotamus; Bernard, Mr. Pennywhistle's dog; Cornelius the Walrus; and Homer.

As the years rolled on, Dennis became more and more involved with the animals, helping Mr. Green Jeans share interesting information about the creatures with the children at home. In Busch Gardens, Florida, Dennis rides a tortoise, seeks advice from a baboon, and gets nuzzled by a camel. At Sea World in California, he shows the Captain how to feed squid to the Walrus.

79

Gus played opposite me as Willy to my Wally... or was it the other way around? He also got to play a variety of roles in scenes with our guest celebrities, such as a bumbling waitress with Alan and Adam Arkin; an ice cream-eating knight with Jordan Clark; and Little Jack Horner opposite Celeste Holm.

Here Gus, playing a
court artist, pretends to
do a royal portrait of
the lovely queen, Estelle
Parsons, but can only
draw his favorite bunny
character. Christine
Ebersole looks more
convincing as Little Bo
Peep than Gus does as a
little old lady. Gus and
Lumpy join John Schuck
as Three Men in a Tub.

Although he was often cloaked behind many of his characters, Gus was as significant a player on "Captain Kangaroo" as Lumpy or myself. His amazing creativity prompted his developing and playing more roles and characters than any other person on the show.

Previous page
Animal visitors graced the Treasure House every day of the show. Mr. Green Jeans, the Captain, and Dennis shared valuable information about these creatures and their habitats. In all, children and parents were introduced to more than 2,000 species of animals—a veritable Captain's Ark!

A Zoo Comes to You

With the ink still wet on her degree in zoology, Ruth Mary Manecke was hired by the famous Bronx Zoo and assigned to the education department. She worked in the school lecture series, bringing animals and knowledge of them to schools, hospitals, and various groups around New York, Connecticut, and New Jersey. It was 1953, and television was just burgeoning. Soon television programs—and there were not a lot of them—were asking Ruth to appear on their shows with her animals.

In 1954, at twenty-three years old, Ruth accepted an offer from WABC-TV in New York to host her own live show, "Animal Fun Time." As Miss Ruth the Pet Shop Lady, she shared all kinds of animals with guest children during the late afternoons, Monday through Friday. This was the same television station that aired "Uncle Lumpy's Cabin" with Lumpy Brannum (Mr. Green Jeans) and my own clown show, "Time for Fun." Gus Allegretti (later the Captain's puppeteer and Dennis the Apprentice) was performing for "Rootie Kazootie" on the ABC network. What diverse talent all under one roof!

Although Ruth continued to work at the Bronx Zoo while doing her TV show, she eventually formed her own animal modeling company to supply animals to television, print, movies, and stage. She has supplied animals for many events, including the pink elephant that Lucille Ball rode down Schubert Alley in a TV special, and for many shows, from the "Today" show to the "Tonight" show. Even now, many of the animals seen on soap operas and in magazines and catalogs—from dogs and cats to snakes and scorpions—are supplied by Ruth Manecke.

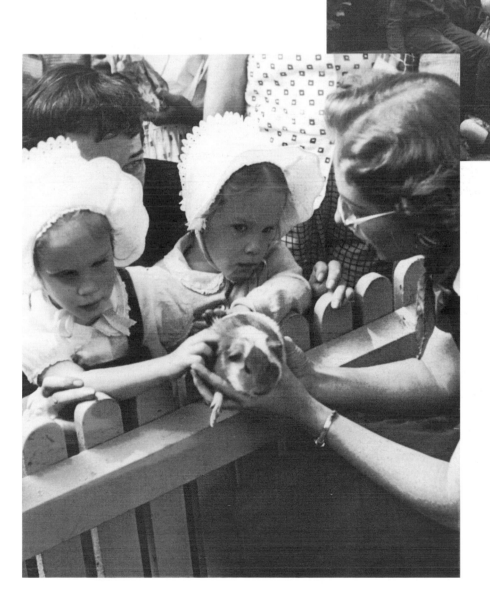

Ruth Manecke, the show's staff zoologist, started her career in the education department at the Bronx Zoo. She shared her knowledge of all kinds of animals with children at the zoo, in hospitals, schools, and groups around the area.

In 1954 and 1955, Ruth supplied and handled the animals for my show "Tinker's Workshop." When "Captain Kangaroo" began in October 1955, Ruth was our only choice as the staff zoologist and animal supplier for all the animals that shared the Treasure House and its gardens.

From the farm version to the exotic, animals were always an important part of our show. These shots of a lamb, a chick, a honey bear (kinkajou), and a goat are from the very first "Captain Kangaroo" show on October 3, 1955.

Our first studio was on the second floor of Leiderkrantz Hall where there was no elevator for transporting props, sets, or animals directly to the set. This posed interesting challenges for getting some of the larger animals to the set. Going up the stairs or climbing was a little more natural for our friends than coming down!

Getting animals downstairs from our secondfloor studio was always a challenge. Here I've borrowed Bunny Rabbit's carrots to coax a donkey back down to the first floor. Imagine this with an elephant or a camel—it happened!

We had a great
diversity of animals to
share, such as monkeys,
llamas, and parrots.

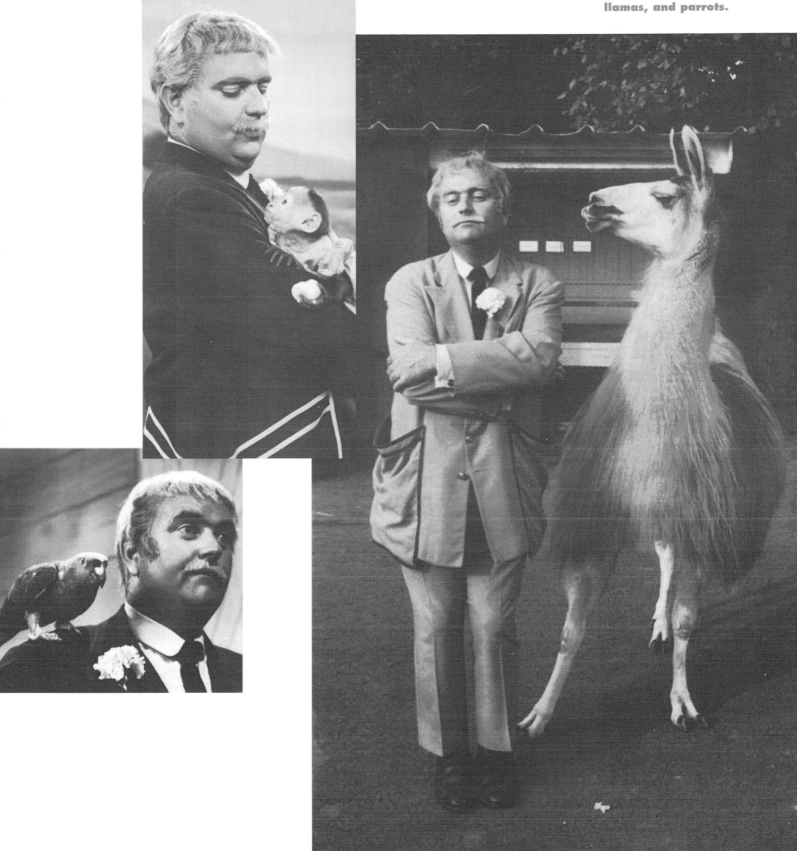

Ruth's degree and knowledge were valuable to the show, but equally as important was her experience with animals while growing up. Ruth's grandfather, Philipp Manecke, Sr., was a renowned surgeon who had an avid interest in the animal world. Beginning early in the century at his home in Brooklyn, Dr. Manecke maintained a small, private zoo replete with birds, monkeys, and snakes. As a young girl, Ruth learned about these animals and how to care for them. Later, Ruth and her father, Philipp Manecke, Jr., did much of the same raising and caring for all kinds of animals. Ruth and her father would receive calls from animal importers asking them to care for desperately ill baby animals. They thought the animals' treatment was outrageously inhumane, from their capture in the wild to their transportation. Yet they knew that if they did not try to save them, the animals would likely die.

Ruth established a clinic and nursery in her own home. Together with her father, she attended to the critical and daily needs of these animals, nursing many of them back to health from the brink of death. These animals included everything from displaced baby squirrels, raccoons, owls and other birds, to orangutans, gorillas, lions, and cheetahs.

Ruth at home with a young gorilla friend, Mr. Pip.

Ruth's father and grand-
father, Philipp Manecke,
Jr. and Sr., were both
naturalists and animal
lovers who influenced
Ruth's interest in
animals from a very
young age.

The animals were cared for and treated 'round the clock like the fragile infants they were. At Ruth's home, it was not unusual to see a young orang or gorilla playing in the trees, wrestling with the family dog, or being bottle fed in caring arms. Many of these animals subsequently appeared on the show.

Ruth has always had a great affection for orangutans. She nursed Bobo back from near-death as an infant and served as his surrogate mother for five years. Bobo became a regular at the Treasure House and here celebrates his first birthday with his friend Susie.

Ruth's favorite was an orangutan named Bobo whom she raised from infancy and cared for for five years. He started out his life extremely ill, and Ruth nursed him back to life, becoming his surrogate mother. Bobo lived with Ruth and had his own car seat, complete with steering wheel and horn for their trips into the city. Bobo loved handing the coins to the toll collectors. Believe it or not, they rarely noticed the long hairy red arm!

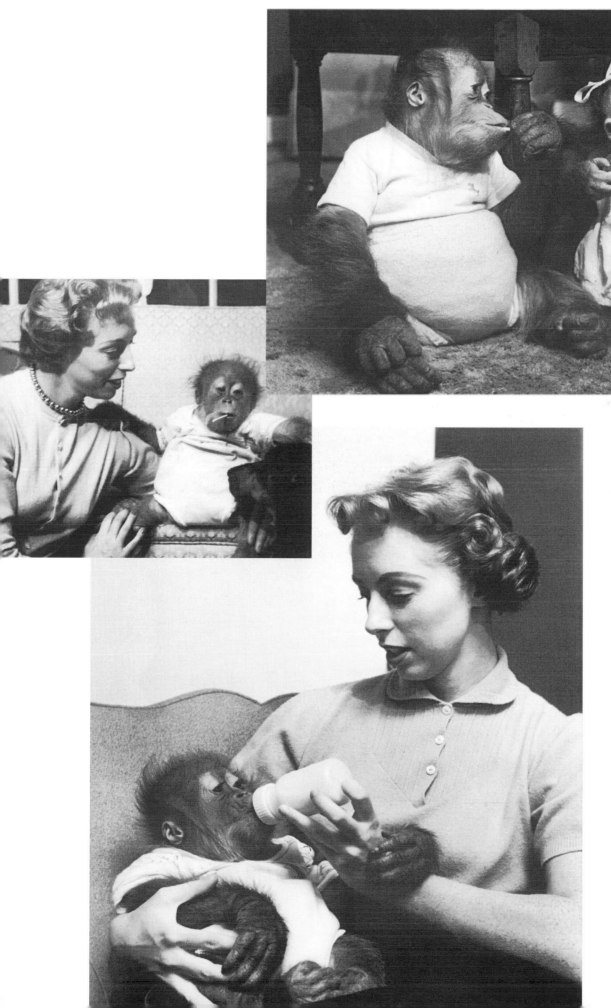

Many animals on the show were Ruth's personal pets. Here Bobo is treated to lollipops and a bottle —just like any youngster!

97

Ruth's daughters, who grew up proud of their mother's work, affectionately tease Ruth that Bobo was her first real child and often wonder why there are home movies of only Bobo and none of them! Giving up Bobo at five years old to go to a Wisconsin zoo was truly traumatic for Ruth.

Another wonderful pet that grew up with Ruth and became a visitor on the show was a mountain lion (or cougar) named Cougie. As a baby, he was a sweet little kitten, but when he grew up and out of his spots, he became a *very* playful cat. One day on the air, when Cougie was a lot bigger, I sat down on the Treasure House steps with my back to him (which Ruth had warned me not to do). Cougie playfully pounced on

Sending five-year-old Bobo to a zoo was as traumatic for Ruth as losing a child. Here they share a tender moment as they prepare to board the plane for the zoo in Racine, Wisconsin.

The baby cougar Cougie was a darling spotted kitten. Ruth always warned me not to get down on his level and turn my back to him. Cats will be cats, but boy! Was my wig ever a mess after that playful encounter!

me from behind, and a tug-of-war ensued during which I tried to coolly hold my wig on my head by gripping my sideburns and Cougie exuberantly tried to pull it off to play! It was the only time in the thirty-plus years of the show that Ruth almost walked on camera. I guess we all have times when we should listen better.

Show biz is not always as glamorous as it seems. Here I share my dressing room as Ruth bathes a squealing piglet in the sink. Incidentally, the bottle on the counter also belonged to the piglet!

One of Bobo's favorite games, besides being tickled, was playing in the water. Here he washes his hands before going on the set. The best (and wettest) part was shaking dry!

As with other show preparations behind the scenes, much more work went into the care of the animals than one would imagine. From feeding and bathing to transportation to and from the set, Ruth always put the animals' needs first.

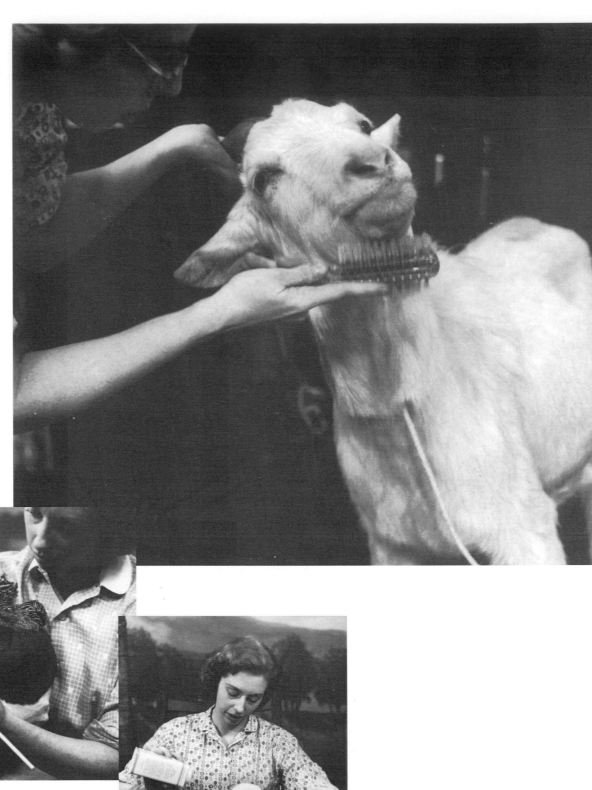

Like many other animals, Beebee the Treasure House dog was one of Ruth's family's personal pets. Beebee was such a "regular" that Ruth would release her down at the CBS loading ramp, and Beebee would run down the hall, past the guards, into the elevator, and off on the second floor where we taped the show.

Beebee the Treasure House dog also grew up on the set. In our days on live television, Beebee served as a "pad" and was called in to play with the Captain to fill a minute or two.

Ruth always reminded us that these were wild animals, even if they had been hand raised. None of the animals on the show were ever tranquilized, and situations were not created to cause harm to animals or humans. The only incident we ever had in all the years was when Lumpy got lightly nipped by a lion cub when the cub's claws got stuck in his sweater.

Ruth also believed in observation—if an animal is going to act out, it will give you some type of sign. She felt that animals were as unpredictable as children. You can't count on them to do what you want when you want, so we were prepared for anything!

Ruth always emphasized a respect of wild animals, even if they were hand raised. She also believed in watching for cues as to when they have had enough. Just like kids!

When laws were finally changed to prohibit the import of animals except to a licensed purchaser, zoo, or animal park, Ruth supervised the selection of and visits to special places for taping "animal spots." She also naturally evolved into producer of the show, as well as the producer of "The Subject Is Young People" radio show.

More than 2,000 species of animals appeared on "Captain Kangaroo." They ranged from farm animals to great apes, exotic reptiles to wild cats. Over the years, Ruth's knowledge of and respect for the animal world have been passed on to millions of children and parents through the Captain, Mr. Green Jeans, and Dennis the Apprentice. For it was Ruth who not only shared this valuable information but showed us how to handle the beautiful creatures we shared with all of you.

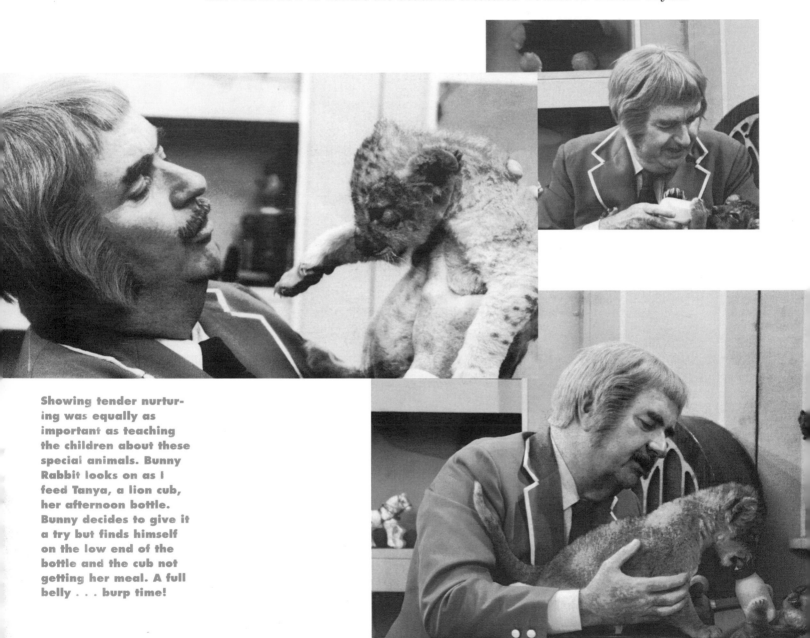

Showing tender nurturing was equally as important as teaching the children about these special animals. Bunny Rabbit looks on as I feed Tanya, a lion cub, her afternoon bottle. Bunny decides to give it a try but finds himself on the low end of the bottle and the cub not getting her meal. A full belly . . . burp time!

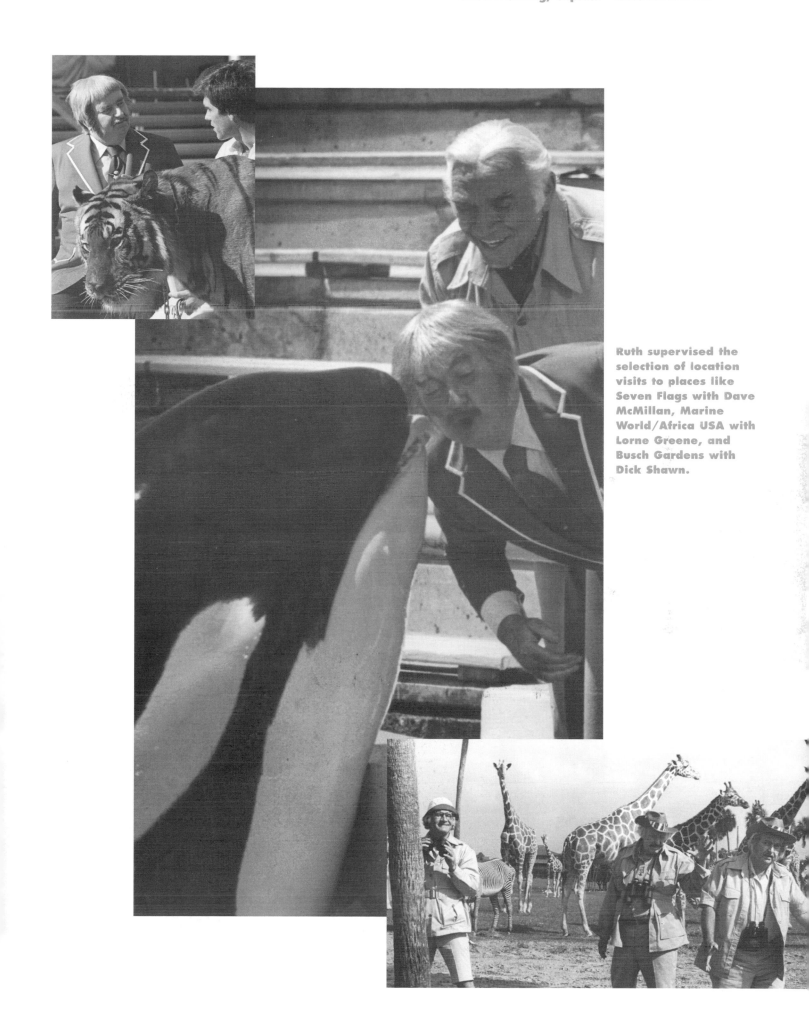

Ruth supervised the selection of location visits to places like Seven Flags with Dave McMillan, Marine World/Africa USA with Lorne Greene, and Busch Gardens with Dick Shawn.

Here I am at Great Adventure Park in New Jersey, making friends with a fellow kangaroo.

Ruth and Lumpy share a laugh over the cute grunts of this chubby bulldog.

From wild to domestic, from jungles to back yards, Ruth's knowledge of and respect for animals were passed on through "Captain Kangaroo" for almost forty years.

Previous page
In our commitment to
give our audience the
best of the best, we had
great fun enlisting the
help of many talented
actors, actresses, and
performers from all
walks of show business.
Through them, we gave
children funny, educa-
tional, and entertaining
skits at the Treasure
House and at locations
around the country.
Here is our good friend
Andy Griffith as a
cowboy on location with
us in California.

The Stars that Shone

M any show business greats performed on "Captain Kangaroo" through the years. People often asked why we called upon such fine performers from television, stage, motion pictures, dance, and music to join us on the program. Was it for their billboard value, an inducement for young people to look in and join the fun?

Of course not. Most of the people who came from these many show business worlds were relatively unknown to young children, as famous as they were in the adult world. Oh, some parents may have been lured to view the program, but we never assembled the program for adults. We were very happy to have the approval of adults and hoped that we were partnering with them in contributing to their children's nurturing.

No, our famous guests from so many fields were invited for one reason. It is my belief that children deserve the best performance possible, and these artists were supreme in performing their art. Simple as that: give children the very best. Be it Eli Wallach, Dolly Parton, Celeste Holm, Geraldine Fitzgerald, Milton Berle, Jack Gilford, Pearl Bailey, Mike Farrell, Danny Aiello, Paul Sorvino, Jerry Stiller, or Anne Meara— from whatever field, these were artists who performed to the highest standard.

Too many producers and television executives feel that a child audience is inferior in its ability to judge performance. "It's only a kid show," is an expression I have heard far too often in a business that often denigrates young audiences. Never on "Captain Kangaroo." Our audience demanded and deserved the best. With these many great artists, they were given the best.

Milton Berle, actor and comedian

"*On this your fiftieth anniversary, I want to congratulate you and wish you happiness and good health for many years to come. You have for the last five decades presented us with clean, wholesome, and educational entertainment.*

"*I loved appearing with you on your show. You are a giant credit to show business.*"

Dolly Parton, singer

"*As a baby boomer, I'm part of the first generation of Captain Kangaroo kids. Now, I was on TV before my family ever owned one, but I was still a fan. As an adult, I become a 'closet' 'Captain Kangaroo' watcher. Being a fan, I was thrilled when Bob asked me to be on his show and was thrilled again when he agreed to be a guest of mine. Now, I've sung many duets in my career, but the only time I ever sang harmony to 'a-boop, boop, did'um, dad'um, wad'um, shoop' was with the Captain. We sang 'Three Little Fishes,' and I got so caught up in his joyful perfor-mance that I couldn't remember my part! That was about twenty years ago, but I will never forget it because I got to work with a man I greatly admired.*

"*Congratulations, Bob, and thank you for fifty wonderful years of sweet and gen-tle children's television. You truly 'swam and you swam right over the dam!' I will always love you.*"

Mike Farrell, actor

"One of the glorious fringe benefits associated with being part of a hit television series, as I was lucky enough to be with M*A*S*H, is the opportunity to join the casts of other shows as a 'guest star.' Of all those offered during my years as 'BJ,' I think the appearances I took the most pride in and had the most fun with were those with Bob Keeshan's Captain Kangaroo. Bob's style of gentle good humor and crazy-but-always-positive fun was the perfect antidote, from my perspective, to the high-speed, jarring, too-often violent fare that has passed as children's programming on television. Whenever I came to the show I knew that my children were always welcome as well, and Bob's happy nature was visible everywhere—in his behavior and in that of everyone else on the set—whether dealing with my kids or with anyone else.

"A happy memory of that time stays with me today as, when I work in my garden, either my wife or one of my children (now grown) will inevitably refer to me as Mr. Green Jeans."

Phyllis Diller, comedienne

"It was such fun being a guest on Bob's show. We have a great deal in common, since we both started out in 1955. He is a dear man—the kind to be a role model for children.

"Years later we were both guests on 'Hollywood Squares' where we discussed my face job and whether he should have one."

Fred Rogers, "Mister Rogers' Neighborhood"

"*Even though Bob and I visited each other's on-air 'neighborhoods,' we know one another best off the air. For instance, we have a tradition of talking on the phone, no matter where we are in the world, every New Year's Day. We've had those New Year's conversations for more than thirty years! We feel it's a good way to start each year.*

"*This past January 1, we talked about our grandchildren; and, of course, child advocacy, which Bob has always helped to further. It's just a fact that Bob Keeshan is a wonderful human being who has made, and continues to make, an important difference in the lives of American children. I'm glad that he and I grew up—on and off television—together.*"

Gwen Verdon, actress

" '*Captain Kangaroo' was 'true make-believe,' which I just love. One year I worked with a tiny fuzzy gray kitten. I loved him so much I took him home. On his first birthday, I went back to the show for his birthday party. He is now called 'FATRICK.' He actually licked the icing off the cake. What fun!*"

Ruth Buzzi, comedienne

"We all know it was some time ago that I guested on the show with Bob on 'Captain Kangaroo.' I do remember going down to San Diego to meet everyone and taping the show at the zoo and having an absolutely fabulous time!!! One of the several things I had to do was stand near the edge of the 'special stand' and allow Shamu to jump out of the water and take a snippet of food out of my hand. From my angle, my hand blended right in with the snippet of food, and if hand and snippet looked all like one to me, HOW could this mammoth mouth bound out of the water and take ONLY THE SNIPPET!!! It was scary, folks. I can remember everyone, especially Bob, cheering me on!!! Oh!! Very concerned was I!!! So, because of the time lapse, I can remember having a great time, loving Captain Kangaroo, and being frightened to death I might fly away from there minus a RIGHT SIDE!!! Ha! Ha!

"Congratulations, Bob!! I'll NEVER forget you!!!"

Eli Wallach, actor

"As my children were growing up, they begged, pleaded, and urged me to do the Captain Kangaroo show. I was lucky to be able to carry out their wishes. I appeared a good number of times with Bob Keeshan playing the role of 'Trader Eli'—loved the role—and found that I was a hero to my children. Bob Keeshan is a hero to me, and to a great portion of the American TV viewing public. All best wishes to him."

Earl "The Pearl" Monroe, New York Knicks

"It was a real pleasure to appear on the Captain Kangaroo show. Remembering the old shows in the fifties and sixties made it extra special. Getting to do a scene with Mr. Green Jeans was a real highlight. As I look back on my appearance on the show, I realize now how much history was involved and the many children it touched. Thank you, Bob Keeshan ... Oh, I mean Captain Kangaroo ... (Clarabell)?"

Barnard Hughes, actor

"I started watching 'Captain Kangaroo' with my children and remained a fan myself. I remember my brief involvement in the show as a complete delight. Being in it was as much fun as watching it. They speak of the Golden Days of Television—Captain Kangaroo was there leading the parade."

Kevin Dobson, actor

"You were always a good example with a good message for the good people. Thank you for letting me be a part of it. I had a great time playing Mr. Fix-it."

John Ritter, actor

"My mom took me to see Captain Kangaroo one day when I was a kid. I must have seen Bob without his jacket, because I said 'That's not the real Captain Kangaroo!'

"Since then, I've had the opportunity to work with Bob on several occasions, and I've never seen anybody work with cue cards the way he does. He's terrific at memorizing—he's the cue card guy! I've always had a great time working with Bob."

Jerry Stiller, actor, and Anne Meara, actress

"Back in the days when we were strictly an act on the 'Ed Sullivan Show,' you asked us to be on the Captain Kangaroo show. As parents of Ben and Amy Stiller, we watched you connect with the minds of young people on a level that to this day has never been equaled.

"Being on your show brought us to the attention of a new audience. Ben and Amy also got to see us and perhaps understood for the first time that our dressing up in funny outfits was okay.

"Congratulations on your miraculous ground-breaking achievements in children's television. You will always be alive and well in our hearts.

"We love you."

Singer and actress Carol Channing

Singer Pearl Bailey

Television anchorman Walter Cronkite

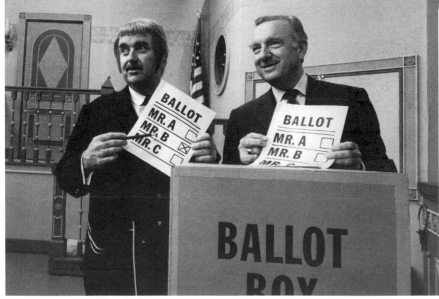

120

Actress Lynn Redgrave

Comedian and actor Bill Cosby

Comedian Arte Johnson

Actress Teri Garr

Actor Danny Aiello

Comedian Soupy Sales

Comedian Tommy Smothers

Actor Alan Arkin

Comedienne Minnie Pearl

Actor/talk show host John Davidson and singer Tony Orlando

Country singer Barbara Mandrell

Actor Jack Gilford

Olympic gold medalist Bruce Jenner

Actresses Penny Marshall and Cindy Williams

Football player Rosie Grier

Sign language performers Julianna Field and Timi Near

Actor Paul Sorvino

Actress Geraldine Fitzgerald

Baseball player Lou Brock

Opera singer Roberta Peters

Talk show host Phil Donahue

Singer and actress Edie Adams

Actress and author Carrie Fisher

Comedienne Peggy Cass

Actress and dancer Chita Rivera

Actress Imogene Coca

Actor Walter Slezak

Actress Lucie Arnaz

Actor Lou Jacobi

Comedienne Joan Rivers

131

Actress and singer Petula Clark

Comedienne Joanne Worley

Actor Hal Linden

Actor and musician Dudley Moore

Singer and actress Melba Moore

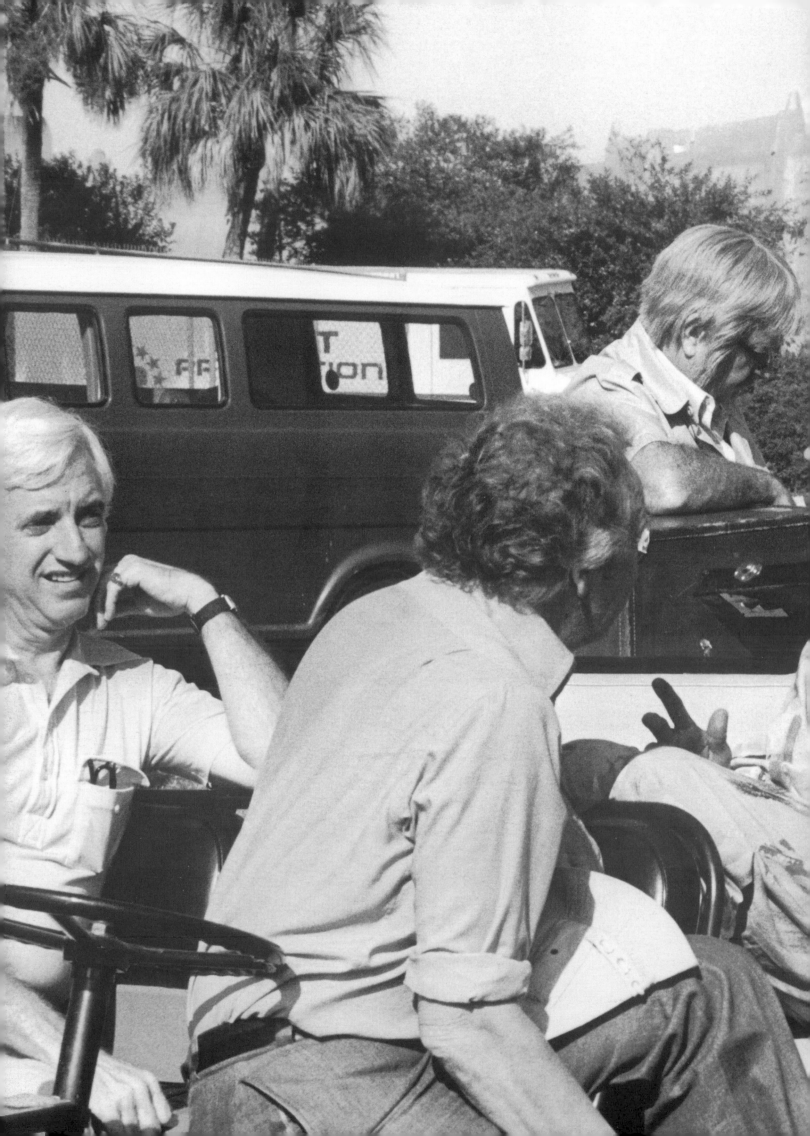

The People Who Made It Happen

Write Me a Script!

I have always believed that every television program begins with writing. The greatest actors, producers, or directors cannot overcome a bad script. Writing is *the* basic ingredient. We were very fortunate to have worked with many fine writers on "Captain Kangaroo," and their contributions were the foundation on which all other talented people could build.

Bob Colleary was one of the early builders of the program. Bob had a wonderful quirky mindset that enabled him to write the best comedy *and* the most sensitive situations. He was an expert on Bunny Rabbit. He worked with Gus Allegretti to create Mister Moose. He knew the location of Dancing Bear's cave, knew what Mr. Bainter liked for lunch, knew what kept Grandfather Clock awake for forty seconds straight. He had an incredible feel for every character. Bob soon became more than a writer; he became our head writer. As such, he developed, taught, and encouraged many talented people to write for "Captain Kangaroo."

Tom Whedon was one such writer, a thoughtful, very intelligent man with a fabulous sense of humor. His Harvard education made him a most literate writer, and he created many outstanding scripts. Bob Brush worked with me on the production of

Writer Bob Colleary collaborates with Gus Allegretti on the development of a new puppet character. This whale was used when the show went aboard the S.S. Treasure House in the summer of 1959.

some children's records. As a writer on our show, he graced us with some terrific operettas, such as "Finnerty Flynn." Jeff Moss was a quiet, laid-back human being who was a part of the "Captain Kangaroo" family from the beginning. His scripts were thoughtful and, most importantly, they worked. Howard Friedlander, Matt Robinson, Claire Labine, Carolyn Miller, Winnie Holtzman, Linda Klein—all these folks created many wonderful scripts for us over the years. And working for "Captain Kangaroo" was only the beginning for many of our writers. Some of their further credits included sit-coms such as "The Cosby Show," "Benson," "The Golden Girls," "Slap Maxwell," and "The Wonder Years"; news magazine shows such as "FYI"; dramas such as "Kung Fu"; and various soap operas. If some of these television shows seem like odd transitions—well, good writing is good writing. How did we manage to assemble so many nice *and* talented people to work on one show?

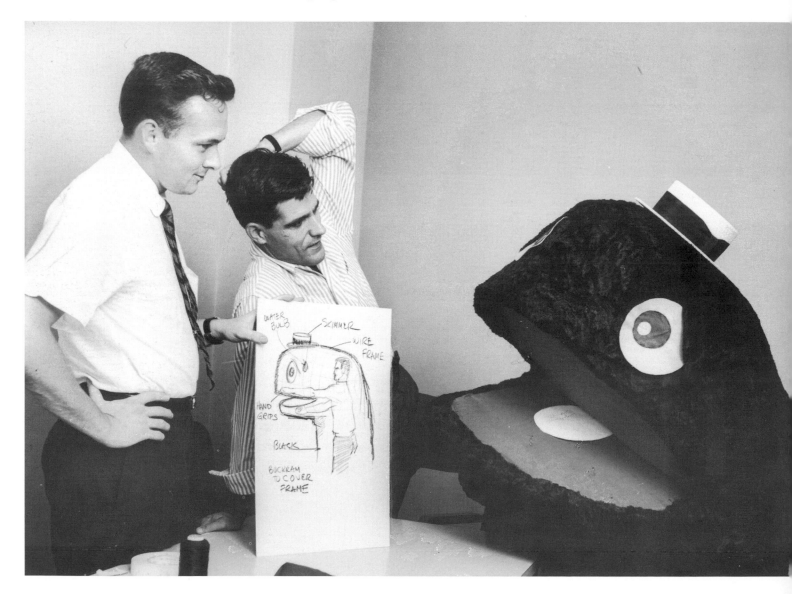

A story development
session with actors,
writers, and producers.
I am the man standing
on the left; Lumpy is
standing on the right.
Don't we all look
young?

Sing Me a Song!

One evening in the early years of the show, Clark "Corky" Gessner, always soft spoken, approached me somewhat tentatively and pressed a large envelope on me. He explained that he had written some songs and would be pleased if I could find time to give them a listen. Oh boy, thought I, how am I going to let this kid down easily? I listened to his tapes that evening and was enthralled. It was some of the finest, most creative work I had ever heard. Within days, Corky was a writer on the show working with Bob Colleary. What scripts and what music he gave us!

Music has always been integral to "Captain Kangaroo," and many fine composers enriched our mornings. Susan Birkenhead wrote song after song and now contributes to much of the music on Broadway. Henry Krieger went on to write "Dream Girls" and "The Tap Dance Kid." Many will remember Lucy Simon from "The Secret Garden." Lynn Ahrens, who wrote "A Christmas Carol" for television and "The Hunchback of Notre Dame" for Broadway, wrote our latest theme song, "Here Comes Captain Kangaroo." Jeff Moss, Bob Brush, Don Siegal, Stan Davis—all wrote great music for us.

Celebrity guests, (here Carol Channing), show regulars, and behind-the-scenes people all helped in studying scripts and preparing cue cards.

Produce Me a Show!

The top production person on any television show is the producer or, more often nowadays, the executive producer. "Captain Kangaroo" was a collaborative effort from day one. Of course, as the creator of the character and much of the show's philosophy, I wielded great influence, but would I not be foolish if I failed to find leadership to coordinate our efforts to produce quality television for young people?

In the beginning, our producer was my partner, Jack Miller. Jack had considerable experience as a producer in Chicago. We met when he was sent to New York to produce my WABC-TV program "Time for Fun," and he also helped me when "Tinker's Workshop" went on the air in the autumn of 1954. When CBS Television decided to offer us the morning time as "Captain Kangaroo," Jack Miller moved to CBS with me as my partner.

Those original days and weeks were busy times. We put together the cast, engaged writers and production personnel, hired secretarial staff and other support forces. We also set show policies, designed costumes and sets, and chose CBS people who would be assigned to us exclusively. Jack Miller was responsible for leading this effort and made many decisions that set the show on its course for many years. He left the program in 1958, and Bob Claver moved up to become producer.

I had met Bob Claver when my WABC-TV show "Time for Fun" went on the air in September 1953. Bob was as easy going a chap as I had ever met. As "Time for Fun's"

Makeup artist Bill Herman and costume manager Hugh Holt help prepare me for production in this rare shot from the early days of the show.

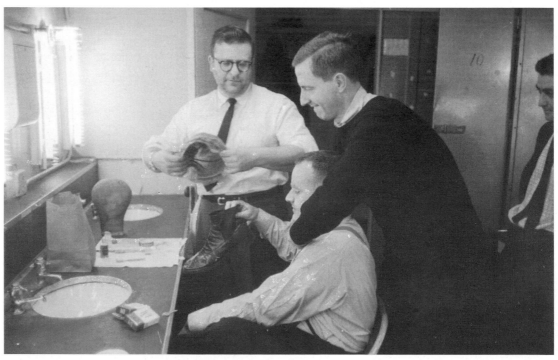

producer, he listened to my ideas for the show and allowed me to try virtually all of them. I suppose I was outrageous because I had strong feelings about the quiet tenor of the program and the gentle lessons my character, Corny the Clown, could bring to his audience. Bob had a wonderful, somewhat dry, sense of humor and encouraged similar traits in me. The experience was wonderful and helped my reputation and my craft.

When Jack Miller and I were putting "Captain Kangaroo" together, it made so much sense to ask Bob to be the associate producer. Bob also had talents as a writer, and many of the ideas for the early programs, most of them ad-libbed around an outline, came from him. A few years later, Bob was offered a post as the producer of a variety program, and because he enjoyed variety television, he accepted.

Bob's replacement, David Brown, always seemed befuddled about why he was chosen to produce "Captain Kangaroo." CBS was more comfortable with an experienced producer, and David certainly had more experience than most people working in television at that time. He was very quiet, soft-spoken, and always *asked* people to

Practically every show member started with cue cards, and everyone pitched in when necessary. Here I am holding cue cards for those on the set.

do things where many other producers might *tell* them. After a year, David Brown went back to programming, and David Connell moved into the producer's post.

Not long after that, it became apparent that the show needed more depth in talent to achieve our goals, and David Connell was made executive producer. We were getting to be like a *real* television program with all these talented people! David remained as executive producer until 1968, when he left to become executive producer of a new enterprise, Children's Television Workshop, and a new program called "Sesame Street."

Producer Jon Stone had the highest of standards for production and an unshakable belief in influencing children with the best in programming. Jon helped form a team essential to the live concert performances we did with symphony orchestras across the nation. (For a few years we did more than twenty concerts a year, *really* exhausting work. But we were, oh, so young!)

Cue cards, puppeteers, technicians, actors, producers, and cameramen all "take five" between scenes.

Producers Al Hyslop and Jim Krayer followed, and they continued to uphold the show's high production standards. Jimmy Hirschfeld had many years of local television experience and a solid background as a director in NFL football coverage before he joined us as a producer. Joel Kosofsky was our unit manager, an associate producer, a producer, and finally supervising producer, managing our budgets and facilities and traveling with me on personal appearances. Bette Chichon, who had joined us many years earlier as a production assistant, became a producer responsible for much of our preproduction and scripts. Ruth Manecke, who had been our zoologist since the very first show, became our studio producer and managed our actual taping sessions.

Sam Gibbon was an associate producer and our studio producer. Sam is a natural teacher, thoughtful, creative, and with a keen insight into the needs of young people and how to meet those needs. Harry Crossfield was a writer and an associate producer in charge of our studio. Harry's keen sense of humor broke many a moment of tension on diffi-

Producers Joel Kosofsky, Jimmy Hirschfeld, Ruth Manecke, and I all meet to discuss a script.

cult taping days. The relationship between the studio producer and the cast and production crew is a vital one, and Harry was able to pull it all off.

Frank Abatemarco came to us to hold cue cards and stayed around to be a production assistant and an associate producer. A pipe, usually unlit, would dangle from his mouth as he proposed instructions to cast and crew. He *proposed* instructions; Frank was too gentle to order anything. Bruce Barry also came to our show to hold cue cards, became a production assistant, and then, for a time, our associate director. Occasionally Bruce directed the show, and today he is an outstanding director for "Guiding Light."

One of our associate producers was a friendly, smiling chap named Norton Wright. Norton had an attractive habit of deliberately mixing adjectives and adverbs. "Good morning, Norton. How are you today?" "I am goodly, thank you, Bob, goodly!" On a made-for-television movie recently, I noticed Norton listed as producer alongside Bob Banner. Working with that cordial gentleman and television pioneer is something to respect. Goodly for you, Norton!

Many "Captain Kangaroo" alumnae went on to other shows, and a great many went on to work for Children's Television Workshop: David Connell, Jon Stone, Al Hyslop, Sam Gibbon, Corky Gessner, Jeff Moss. I am proud of all those who joined CTW, proud of the influence they have had on quality children's television.

Behind the Camera

Peter Birch was the original director of "Captain Kangaroo," and in the more than twenty years he occupied the control room, Peter set the style and substance of much of the program.

Peter, a Manhattan kid, started his professional career as a dancer and performed in many Broadway productions. He was a protégé of the great Agnes De Mille, and it is said that she was so entranced with his dancing that she assigned him dancing

This unusual shot shows the production team behind the "scenes" on location at Sea World with celebrity guest Ruth Buzzi.

Peter Birch began directing "Captain Kangaroo" in 1955 and continued with the show for more than twenty years. Like many valuable and valued directors, Peter set the tone and determined the content for much of what appeared on the show.

roles in two Broadway shows simultaneously. Peter would dance in act one of "Carousel" and then go quickly to an adjacent theater to dance in act two of "Oklahoma."

In looking for a director for the soon-to-be Captain, I was impressed by Peter's understanding of performance and felt confident that he would appreciate the challenges presented by the combination of camera movements and actors on stage. Peter came to know my every move before I made it. He gave me a great sense of security, which allowed me to worry about other aspects of the production.

Peter Birch chose much of the music with which millions of children grew up. Children then, as well as now, had little exposure to classical music. Peter filled much of that void in a most entertaining manner. An apt example was Miss Worm singing Verdi in the shower as steam rose from below, eventually obscuring all but her magnificent voice. Peter also helped introduce children to the classical performing arts. Early on, we established the "Treasure House Ballerina," Roberta Lubell, who danced on a regular basis to music that she and Peter chose and choreographed.

A Cast of Characters

When "Captain Kangaroo" first aired in 1955, a few critics pointed out that it had a predominantly male cast. One critic also said that the program was *too* gentle and did not prepare young children for the violence they would encounter in real life! I assured this critic that thousands of producers were hard at work on violent pro-

Peter Birch gives suggestions to Lumpy and zoologist Ruth Manecke before one of our sometimes unpredictable animal segments. Having wild animals on the set was always a challenge for a director!

Opposite
Lovely Roberta Lubell appeared regularly as the "Treasure House Ballerina." Roberta, touchingly, received fan mail from small girls asking how they could become ballerinas and always responded with helpful advice.

gramming and there would be no dearth of such material. What young children *did* need was examples of kindness, of cooperation and accommodation, of using words in problem solving. These were the tools that needed to be modeled.

There was no question that the cast of Lumpy Brannum, Gus Allegretti, and I weighed in favor of males. However, most young children's experience at the time centered on mother and grandmother, women schoolteachers, female baby-sitters, and the numerous teachers of local television programming. I felt strongly a need to balance this overwhelming female presence with strong male role models. Nonetheless, there was no reason why we could not add greater balance to the show.

When the program first went on the air, there was a young viewer in Houston named Debbie Weems who, like other viewers, learned to tell time from Grandfather Clock. Time went by, and Debbie grew. As a young woman she performed on stage, including a principal role in the musical "Godspell." Debbie seemed perfect for a regular female character role. She possessed a sweet voice, a shy personality, good acting ability, and puppeteering talents. Debbie showed young women that they could be anything they desired.

The many faces of Debbie Weems, who grew up watching the show and eventually became part of our family. When playing the cute Baby Duck, Debbie would often comment the duck was "myself as a five-year-old!"

Debbie displays her derring-do in a sketch on location in Busch Gardens, Florida.

Again, the human cast chemistry was most important, and when Debbie joined us it was as though she had been born into our family. She experienced tragedy in her personal life, and all of us felt the greatest of pain when we lost her.

Jane Connell and Bill McCutcheon were two fine stage and television performers who joined "Captain Kangaroo's" cast of regulars in 1965. One of their most famous sketches was the Homan Family, in which Jane was Mrs. Homan, Bill was Mr. Homan, and Gus Allegretti was their son. The Homans were a mixed-up, backwards family who did virtually everything in reverse. They stood up to dinner every morning and, of course, enjoyed breakfast every evening. They mixed up words and meanings and were thoroughly confusing, much to the delight of our audience. Children are learning ordered social patterns, and when these are mixed up, they find it very amusing. Jane and Bill are great comedians and added many fun sketches to the show.

Although the cast had been joined by many guests of minority backgrounds, it also seemed sensible to develop a regular minority character. We auditioned many performers sent by agents and casting directors. Talent was important, but we knew that

Jane Connell and Bill McCutcheon played the hapless Homans, much to the delight of our young audience, who loved to see the mixed-up family do things backwards.

joining our family was also important. Halfway through this audition process I was approached by our long-time stage manager Jimmy Wall, who asked me when he was going to get a crack at the role. I soon found out Jimmy was not only a great stage manager for Walter Cronkite, the U.S. Tennis Open, political conventions, and "Captain," but was also a singer, dancer, and performer on the other side of the camera, having done television, movies, and a few Broadway shows. The audition was a snap—Jimmy was already a family member. He assumed the role of the math teacher, Mr. Baxter, as though it was designed just for him. He had great energy and a warmth that reached the heart of children and their parents.

Carolyn Mignini was a great singer and versatile Broadway and television actress with wonderful comedic talents. In the latter years of the CBS production, Carolyn joined us as our "woman character" and graced us with great performances and good friendship.

Jimmy Wall as the math teacher Mr. Baxter, on the set with Dancing Bear, me, and Mr. Green Jeans. Jimmy has become a strong friend through the years and I treasure his kindness to me. One of the bonuses to our relationship has been getting to know Jimmy's wife, Dolly. My wife Jeanne and she had much in common managing the two per-formers!

Below
Carolyn Mignini joined our family in 1981. She had been a Miss Teen-Ager and could have passed for one at any time!

Right
Puppeteer Kevin Clash poses with one of his creations. (Kevin is the one without the mustache!)

New and old cast members joined together for "Wake Up with the Captain" in the early 1980s. The updated format also included a new hairdo and cardigan for me—no more red jacket! Left to right are Gus Allegretti, Lumpy Brannum, me, Carolyn Mignini, Kevin Clash, and an assortment of Kevin's puppet creations.

For a few years, Kevin Clash was a regular performer with "Captain Kangaroo," working as a puppeteer and actor. Kevin constructed his puppets as well as performed with them. He made puppet characters especially for the show, and they were wonderful! We encouraged Kevin to come out from behind his puppets and play some acting roles. He seemed almost shy when performing without his puppets. He had no need to be; he was a talented actor. Kevin was recognized as a great talent by another great talent, Jim Henson, who brought him to his troupe of Muppets on "Sesame Street."

Opposite
Any successful television show is created by far more people than just those the audience sees on screen. Here are some of the people, from in front of the camera and behind the scenes, who helped make "Captain Kangaroo" possible.

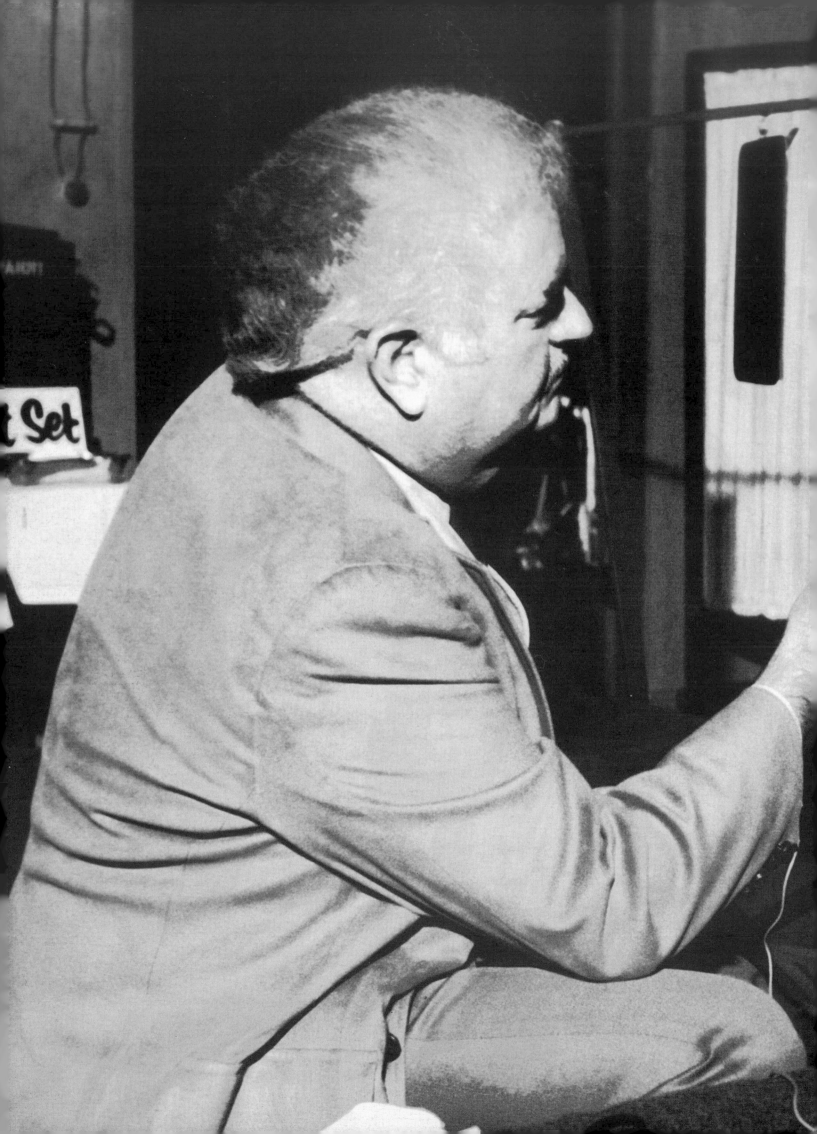

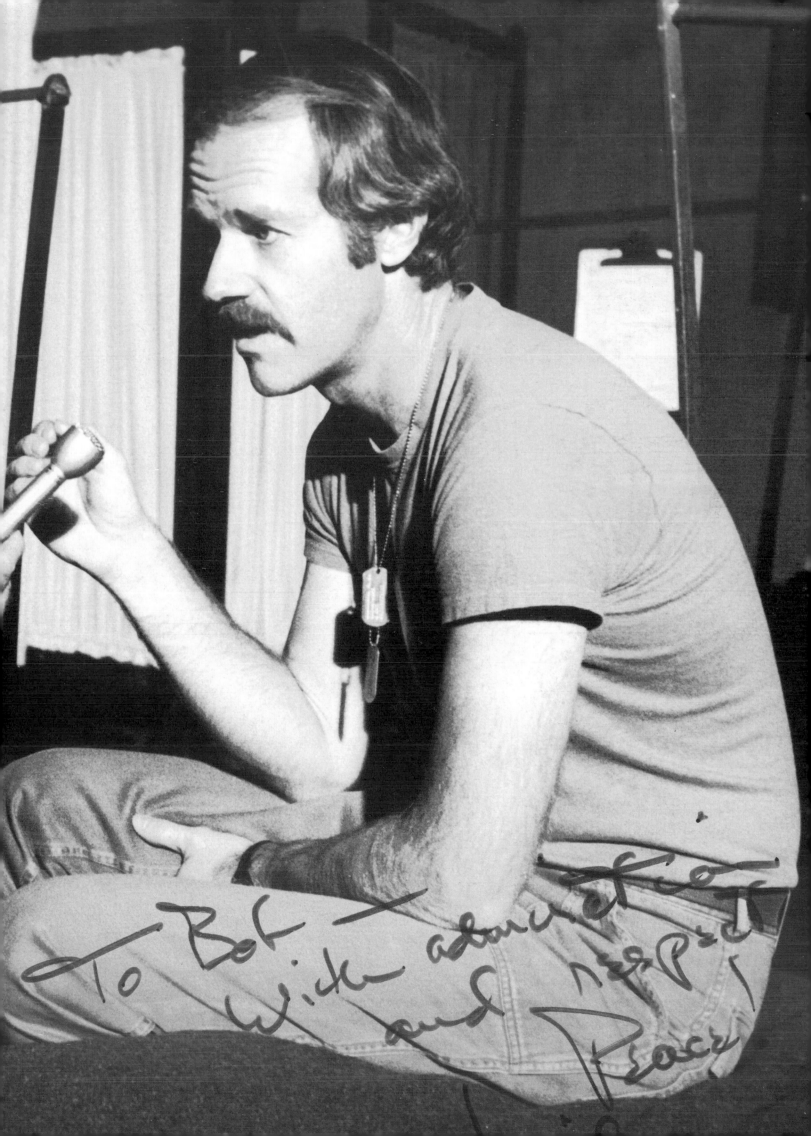

To Bob — With admiration
and respect
David
Peace

Outside the Treasure House

Fun with Music

Most children saw "Captain Kangaroo" on one of the two hundred television stations around the country, but we knew it was important to leave the studio, get into the community, and go to families and children around the nation. Personal appearances helped promote the television program, of course, but it was even more valuable in giving me firsthand contact with the audience, unseen to me in the television format.

However, I was unhappy with the other formats available to me. An appearance in a store or a shopping mall led to large crowds and long waits with great discomfort for young children and their parents. We finally devised a program that maintained the high quality of the television program while still bringing us into contact with many children. This was the Fun with Music series. We worked with symphony orchestras across the nation to meet young children and introduce them to classical music and their local symphony orchestras.

We did not insist on proper decorum from the children—after all, most were under seven years of age. We produced the concert so that it was a visual as well as an audible experience. We would meet the various "families" of the orchestra, much like our own families with its many different siblings and relatives. Meet the string family, violin, viola, cello, and bass violin. The different instruments would play, and we could hear the differences and the unity in the one family.

After introducing the orchestral families, we might talk about George Gershwin and how he created music to sound like a busy street in Paris. As the orchestra played, a dozen children from the audience would join us on stage and climb into open cardboard boxes decorated as autos and trucks and buses. The Captain, properly costumed, would be the gendarme directing the busy traffic.

Our goal for the Fun with Music series was to introduce children to classical music in a fun and interactive way without the restrictions of typical symphony decorum or the distracting pandemonium of a shopping center production. This program is from a visit to the Detroit Symphony Orchestra in 1985.

CAPTAIN KANGAROO

**Detroit Symphony
Young People's Concert Series
March 9, 1985
Earlybirds 11 a.m.
Lazybirds 2 p.m.**

**"Take a tried and true TV hero, add a sparkling symphony orchestra, then mix well with some 6,000 kids, and you have a hilarious, interesting afternoon called 'Fun with Music.' And what fun it was!"
—Oklahoma City Oklahoma-Times**

In the "William Tell Overture," what else…? The children in the audience would ride their horses as though they were the Lone Ranger. Many a theater seat was tested during that music!

In "Flight of the Bumblebee" I would, as the music played, take a net and search for a bumblebee to put in my hive, a medium-sized cardboard box. At the conclusion I would tell the children I had been successful in my quest. Not having actually *seen* the bumblebee, they would deny this. After being hurt that they doubted me (and after having cleverly switched boxes), I would then open the box to release a yellow-jacketed-bee-looking-helium-filled balloon that would rise to the outside of the arch and remain on the concert hall ceiling through the next few orchestra performances.

These marvelous concerts usually ended with me trying to conduct the orchestra. I would ask the conductor for his magical baton, thinking that if he could do it, so

Playing an instrument in the orchestra could not possibly be that difficult, I would insist. I would search for an instrument that wasn't too difficult to play and discover the firebell. To the music of the "Fireworks Polka," I would studiously watch the conductor for my cues, often striking the bell off beat or missing the cues entirely. Although the children got a big kick out of this, the point was made: playing in an orchestra was not something to take casually.

In "Sleigh Ride," by Leroy Anderson, I would bundle up in a huge coat, fur hat, red mittens, long red scarf, and earmuffs, then sit on a stool with reins to accentuate the winter feeling of the music. I would ask the children questions but pretend I couldn't hear them because of the earmuffs. They would squeal with delight when they finally got me to figure out the problem.

could I. I would attempt to conduct, with results that sounded disastrous (which was actually difficult for the musicians to do). Everyone would cover their ears. The conductor would say that it was easy and that the children in the audience could do it. He showed them how to wave their arms up and down, and the orchestra played a magnificent rendition of "Stars and Stripes Forever." Was this ever empowering for the children; they loved it!

As the children in the audience successfully conducted the orchestra (after my own disastrous attempt!), I would march around the stage proudly bearing the American flag.

We played these concerts from the late 1950s to the early 1990s, on weekends and between weekday tapings. A new concert was designed each year because we visited eight or ten of the same orchestras year after year. We played Houston, Detroit, Toronto, Dallas, Denver, and many other major orchestras, plus smaller orchestras in Grand Rapids, Kalamazoo, and other places. We televised concerts from Carnegie Hall, McCormick Place, Chicago, Robin Hood Dell in Philadelphia, and the Hollywood Bowl.

The Carnegie Hall concert occurred just as the new Lincoln Center complex opened and the fate of the renowned Carnegie was in doubt. Governor Nelson Rockefeller had appointed a commission to make recommendations. On the day of the concert, my wife Jeanne was driving our children to the city from our Long Island home. (We owned a station wagon, principally to transport children everywhere, and

Thousands attended this early Hollywood Bowl concert, allowing us the wonderful direct contact with our audience that we loved. Unlike most of our Fun with Music events, this concert was also televised by CBS-TV.

the conversation, as always, was nonstop. Years later Michael commented, "I was an adolescent before I realized that station wagon was a classroom and Mom was the teacher!") They were excited about the concert and halfway through the trip an announcement came on the car radio that the governor's commission had recommended preserving Carnegie Hall. "See!" said Michael from his seat. "Mom, I knew Dad would save Carnegie Hall!" That young man always displayed unlimited faith in me.

The Subject Is Young People

The five-minute radio show "The Subject Is Young People" aired on the CBS Radio Network Monday through Friday from 1979 to 1981. It was a natural outgrowth of "Captain Kangaroo" and my personal philosophy, a concern about young people. On the show, we defined young people as anyone from neonate to twenty-year-old, so the subject matter ranged far and wide.

The show was not designed as strictly "advice to parents," though it occasionally served that purpose. Rather it was designed to be fun, sometimes amusing, but always informative about young people and their needs. We often interviewed guests to elicit opinions and information about children and adolescents. For example, Lee Salk—a respected child psychologist and brother of Jonas Salk, developer of the polio vaccine—talked to us about children in current society and the challenges they faced.

Our guests came from show business, sports, science, medicine, business, education, religion—virtually every field where information and opinions regarding young people could be solicited. The topics discussed were equally diverse—divorce, death, handicaps, medical research, grandparenting, nutrition, television, corporal punishment, child abuse, the cost of college, motivating young people, violence in the home and on the streets, anything to help us raise young people.

The show's viewpoint was that we must *all* be concerned about *all* children, not only our own, because we all pay the social and economic price for nurturing failures. The future, our future, depends on how well we as a society successfully nurture all children.

Our "Captain Kangaroo" zoologist and producer, Ruth Manecke, also produced "The Subject Is Young People"; Sandy Travis was the lead writer. We were recognized with several awards, including the prestigious Gabriel Award in 1982. The program required much time for production, writing, and research, but it was a rewarding effort for us all.

An interview with talk
show host Mike Douglas
for our radio show "The
Subject Is Young People."
Along with Mike and me
is producer Ruth Manecke
and public relations
director Steve Reichl.

A Road Show

By the 1960s, improved videotape technology allowed us to take "Captain Kangaroo" to wonderful places. Taping material in the studio weeks, often months, in advance of an air date afforded us the opportunity to travel. Zoos and wild animal parks were some of our first destinations, and we traveled to San Diego, Busch Gardens, Sea World, and Marineland/Africa USA. We gazed at baby Siberian tigers, gawked at tall giraffes, met Shamu the killer whale, and giggled at porpoises. Visiting such places as The Audubon Zoo in New Orleans, Burnett Zoo in Syracuse, and Great Adventure in New Jersey let us come close to wonderful animals in their free environment and learn much about the creatures with whom we share a planet.

We used vast Opryland and Six Flags settings for wonderful plots acted superbly by our cast and guests from movies, television, music, and stage. We went to Curaçao for "The Missing Paint Mystery," to Costa Rica to load a banana boat, then on to the Panama Canal to follow that same ship and explore that great engineering feat.

We visited many locations around the country and the world, bringing back new cultures and experiences to the children at home. Here a billboard advertises our appearance in Augusta, Georgia; I enjoy the opportunity to cool off on a visit to Curaçao; I chat with two Native American boys at the Minneapolis Aquatennial in 1959; and a young friend shakes hands with Dancing Bear in front of a Dutch barrel organ on a trip to Holland.

As well as having
hundreds of guests visit
the Treasure House, I
occasionally did guest
appearances myself
on the shows of some
friends, including "The
Tony Orlando and Dawn
Show" with Tony
Orlando and some young
friends, "Mister Rogers'
Neighborhood" with
Fred Rogers, and
"Murphy Brown" with
Candice Bergen.

Something to Laugh About

Over the years, innumerable incidents happened both on the camera and off that were very funny. With so many characters on the show, including our own cast, puppet characters, guest celebrities, and location visits all over the globe, it was inevitable that we would have "situations" that we would end up chuckling over either on the spot or in hindsight. What follows are a few of my favorite funny stories, which are all true.

Little Boy Miltie

It was a real thrill for me to work with Milton Berle. When I first came to television, Uncle Miltie *was* television—"Mr. Television," in fact. Buffalo Bob Smith and his sidekick Clarabell made an appearance on his show, "Texaco Star Theater," in those early days. Milton had a very popular character called "Little Boy Miltie"—juvenile attire, short pants, a real brat of a kid. Milton himself was a taskmaster, and in rehearsal, he made it very clear the performance he wanted in every detail. That's what made him such a great performer. Live television allowed no room for retakes, and Milton wanted every scene, every comedy line, every action, to be perfect.

In this skit, Little Boy Miltie was given a birthday party, and Clarabell brought the cake. When the clown was about to cut the cake for the small guests, Little Boy Miltie threw a tantrum and insisted that he "wanted it all." Buffalo Bob pleaded with him to be polite and share, but he continued his tirade: "No, I want the whole thing, the whole thing!" Finally, Buffalo Bob said, "Okay, Clarabell, give him the whole thing!" So Clarabell took the cake and gave him "the whole thing" right in the face. Curtain!

It is amazing that Milton Berle ever agreed to appear on "Captain Kangaroo" after what I did to him on *his* show!

Perfectionist that he is, Milton gave me very careful instructions on how to plaster him with the whipped cream cake. "Bring your arm holding the cake way back, and then, with *full force*, bring it up and hit me right in the middle of my face." This was years of vaudeville skits talking, and I paid careful attention to every detail. After all, this was the master of slapstick comedy.

Air time came, and our skit came near the end of the show. I kept muttering to myself, "Bring the arm way back and hit him right in the face." Unknown to me, however, the prop man had left the whipped cream cake in the metal pan in which he'd made it. Came my cue line, "Okay, Clarabell, give him the whole thing!" and I picked up the pie in my gloved hand, reached back, way back, and wound up. Bam! Perfect! Right in the middle of Milton's face. Huge laughter and a very professional "take" from Milton. Curtain. Only then did I find out that I had hit Milton with the cake, metal plate and all, square on the bridge of his nose!

"He damn near killed me! I'm bleeding, damned kid!" I moved offstage as fast as my huge clown shoes would allow. I was scared to death. Was this the end of my career? Milton, in live television, went on to his next scene.

Years later, when Milton paid us his first visit, I reminded him of the event. He had no memory of it and only asked, "Did we get a big laugh?" In my opinion, he is still "Mr. Television."

The Tale of the Dachshunds

We usually had animal acts on the program on Saturdays, and the acts often came from a circus or a former vaudeville act. Such were the two acrobatic dachshunds who visited us one Saturday.

The act involved two dogs, one of whom positioned himself atop a ladder while the other jumped from a platform onto a seesaw. On the opposite end of the seesaw was a rubber hot dog—a perfect treat for the dachshund, the "hot dog" dog. When the second dog hit the seesaw, the frankfurter was propelled through the air to the top of the ladder and caught by the first dog. The trainer then replaced the hot dog, and the dogs went through the routine again, on and on, through many, many rubber hot dogs.

The trainer told our director that the dogs were tired from their long trip and asked if they could just walk through the act and save the dogs the trouble of rehearsing. Our director, a compassionate man, said, "Of course," and walked his cameras through the routine:

Wide shot, which would show a dachshund jumping on the seesaw.
Tight shot, which would show a dachshund on the ladder catching the
    rubber frank.
Wide shot of dog jumping on seesaw.
Tight shot of dog catching frank, and so on.

We figured we were ready to go on the air for a live broadcast.

Unknown to us, however, these dachshunds were from *early* vaudeville. They were very old, and that little guy on the top of the ladder had lost his teeth. He had to catch those rubber franks with his gums and, bless him, that hurt. So what happened?

On air. Wide shot. Dog jumps on seesaw, frank flies through the air.
Tight shot. Dog *ducks*, and frank flies through the shot!
Wide shot. Dog jumps on seesaw, frank flies through air.
Tight shot. Dog *ducks*, and frank flies through the shot.

And on and on, until the trainer ran out of franks.

If I had known a canine dentist, I would have sent that poor doxie to him straightaway! Our words to the trainer were less than kind. In retrospect, though, that tight shot of the dog ducking and the franks flying by was some of the funniest television I have ever seen!

Opposite
On location in England in the late 1950s. Even Captain Kangaroo could not stir the attention of this diligent guard.

There Will Always Be an England

In the late 1950s, we filmed some material for "Captain Kangaroo" in England. We showed scenes such as the English child's delightful sport of "train spotting." In a day when the British rails dominated that nation's transportation, children would visit various train stations and, notebook in hand, record the numbers and names of engines and passenger cars, along with the date and time of spotting. It was great sport to find a previously spotted engine or passenger car weeks or months later and to compare "spottings" with friends. Our crew also toured the Tower of London, watched the changing of the guard at Buckingham Palace (didn't spot Alice, however), visited Westminster Abbey, and saw many other attractions.

During our visit, I stayed at the grand Savoy Hotel, and each afternoon after a day of filming, I would return to my quarters at the Savoy to find a bucket of ice and refreshments laid out. Each guest had a perfectly British butler/valet who, almost unnoticed, saw to every need. Each evening this valet quietly entered my room and removed the costume I had used in that day's filming. (Remember the oversized jacket with huge pockets trimmed in blue stitching?) He then carefully pressed and cleaned the costume and quietly returned it to my closet.

On the evening before my departure, this wonderful, quiet man spoke to me with great respect. "Begging your pardon, sir. I have been admiring your uniform and would respectfully ask, in which of Her Majesty's regiments do you serve?"

It was a wonderful confirmation of all that was English, so very English!

Another funny story from our time filming in England involved a person unwilling to admit ignorance about almost any subject on earth.

In the late 1950s, "Captain Kangaroo" was not seen in England. One day, on location at the Tower of London with a BBC film crew, we watched the beefeaters and talked about the history of that magnificent attraction. The tower always has tourists and other visitors on hand, and our film crew added to their curiosity.

During the shoot, I became aware of a man who looked like the perfect retired officer from Her Majesty's colonial service—tweed jacket, regimental tie, debonair cap, and pipe. He appeared as if he had just stepped off the boat after a tour of service. He watched intently every move I made, his steady gaze implying great interest.

Our BBC production supervisor, a marvelously efficient lady, told me that during a break in our filming, this chap approached her and crisply asked, "Pardon me, madam, but can you inform me as to the identity of that gentleman in the large blue jacket?"

"Why, yes," she replied, "that is Captain Kangaroo."

"Oh, yes, oh, yes, of course. I should have known. Captain Kangaroo, of course. Rather old to be a Captain, what?"

There will always be an England, thank goodness!

What Made Those Ping-Pong Balls Fall?

One of the questions I am asked most often at book signings or after speeches is "What was the secret word that made the ping-pong balls fall?

There was no one secret word. Everyone in the audience knew what was going to happen, and it *was* fun to see the adult figure of Captain Kangaroo hustled by Mister Moose, often with the assistance of Bunny Rabbit. But it would strain credulity to have the Captain fall for the *same* word every day. Instead, that moose managed to come at me in many, many ways—a poem, a knock-knock joke, a riddle. He might ask

I've always wondered if the audience knew where the ping-pong balls came from. More than Mister Moose and I were involved in each ping-pong ball drop, including the people who had to pick them all up! On location in Atlanta, Gus and I prepare for "the drop." Our stage manager holds up the scene card, while our supervising producer prepares to drop the ping-pong balls. A producer learns to do everything!

Back in 1969, on location in Curaçao, Mister Moose dropped the ping-pong balls on Gus, who was playing a matador. Practice makes perfect!

me to read the poem he was submitting in school that day. As a proper guardian I would do so:

> "Roses are red,
> Violets are blue.
> I like it most,
> When ping-pong balls fall on you!"
> "No, no!" I would protest helplessly, hands above my head, as the dozens of ping-
> pong balls fell, to the delight of all of you at home.
> "Knock, knock."
> "Who's there, Mister Moose?"
> "Alaska."
> "Alaska who, Mister Moose?"
> "Alaska to duck, 'cause here they come!"
> "No! No! Oh, Mister Moose."
> "Hee, hee, hee!"

Dropping those ping-pong balls was a precise exercise in aiming and timing on the part of the stage crew (high up in the grid above me), the stage manager, and the director. As difficult as dropping the balls may have been, *picking up* the balls was the real challenge. More than once, we were grateful for an extra pair of hands supplied by the stage hands' union.

How many ping-pong balls fell in all those years? Who knows? Surely I was too busy to count!

No, Mr. Green Jeans Was Not Frank Zappa's Father!

High on the list of dipsy rumors about "Captain Kangaroo" is that Lumpy Brannum, Mr. Green Jeans, was Frank Zappa's father. Where does such a rumor start? Who knows? Perhaps some disc jockey playing the Zappa song "Wallflowers" suggested that the lyric referring to Mr. Green Jeans may have been a tribute to Lumpy (which it was). From there it could be a short leap to the notion that Lumpy was Frank's father.

Other silly rumors have persisted over the years, including those from people who swear they knew me as a youngster. I lived in two houses for the first twenty years of my life, and the same four families lived next door during all those years. Yet people have told me they know so-and-so who lived next door, and by my last count, over a thousand people lived in those four houses. I went to a high school with only a few hundred students, but I have been told of thousands of people who knew me intimately during those years. Heck, I was so shy I hardly talked to any of my classmates. I remember a few who were kind to the quiet kid that I was.

But people are insistent. They seem to know better than I. I have had people, who seemed to be fairly intelligent, argue with me when I say, "No, that's only a rumor."

Here's the truth: the only son of Lumpy and Peg Brannum is a terrific man named Tom Brannum. The last time I heard of Tom, he was happily pursuing an acting career. Let the rumors rest in peace.

Sorry, Frank.

The Elder Statesman

For a nation that frequently proclaims its love for children, we act in a very strange way. Yes, we love our own children, but often caring about other children is a different matter. America is one of the wealthiest nations on earth, and yet we are the first modern industrial nation to have made children our principal underclass. More than one-fifth of our children live in poverty. How do we expect a bright economic future for this nation when we are willing to discard twenty percent of that future?

I don't talk in terms of compassion any longer; I talk economics because children have become an economic issue, and Americans seem to understand and react to their pocketbooks. Americans must care about children at risk because we all pay the very high cost of failure when we do not. Alcohol, violence, and many other societal ills affecting our nation's youth are very expensive conditions. As taxpayers, we should insist that low-cost preventive programs be introduced to deal with children and families at risk. Only then will we cut into the disastrously high costs of remedial programs, costs that drag on our financial well-being as a nation. It's much like caring for an automobile; preventive maintenance avoids expensive repairs. We develop our children, for better or worse, in their first six years, and a very small expenditure on those at risk during those first years can save lives and benefit our nation.

My personal philosophy of how we ought to act in this world provides the basis for the kind of children's television programming that I do. My programs are based on a respect for children, their intelligence, and their potential good taste. I think that civility and good manners are very important in society. The "in your face, up yours" attitude that many of us display to each other is, I believe, a disaster for America. "Do unto others" as a way of behaving is laughable to many children and adults. Yet this attitude affects our everyday relationships, our politics, our civility. Many adults I meet today who grew up with the Captain will comment on how nice we were to them and to each other. Mr. Green Jeans, Dancing Bear, even Bunny Rabbit and Mister Moose displayed kindness toward each other. This deliberate display of good manners made the Treasure House quite wonderful to inhabit.

Because I've worked with children all my life, it should not surprise anyone that for forty years I have spent much of my time representing children across the country, defending their place in our future and urging us all to work to assure that place. About thirty times each year, I speak to child advocacy groups, educators, law enforcement and judicial officials, corporate human resource directors, lieutenant governors, and local and state legislators. I have testified before Congress on the effects of television on families, on tobacco use by juveniles, and particularly on the

Many times each year, I speak before various child advocacy organizations. In 1993, I addressed parenting issues before an audience of NACHRI members (National Association of Children's Hospitals and Related Institutions).

shaping of attitudes. I testify before agencies such as the Federal Communications Commission, the Federal Trade Commission (about television commercials), and local legislators (about corporal punishment). I speak before people working to prevent the abuse of children, before audiences concerned about the health of children, about violence in the streets and violence in homes. Anything that affects the well-being of children is of keen interest to me.

In the late 1950s, I shared a speaking platform with a young United States senator from Massachusetts. He was at the time a bachelor, but his brother Bobby had a host of children, and the senator wondered if I would meet with them after a concert I was to do the next day with the National Symphony. The meeting was arranged, and it was the first of many delightful times I spent in Virginia with the great family of Bobby and Ethel Kennedy.

Testifying before Senate or Congressional committees is another way I work to support children's issues. During this testimony, I was supported by actors Jonathan Forsythe and Amanda Blake.

Much of my philosophy
is based on respect for
children. I also believe
in business-sponsored,
high quality, develop-
mental child care,
which is why I cofound-
ed a company that
provides such care for
corporations, banks,
and hospitals.

One of the saddest days of my life was in June 1968, sitting in Saint Patrick's Cathedral in New York for the funeral of Bobby Kennedy, senselessly assassinated after winning the California presidential primary. In the days following, I took part in numerous conversations with television executives who were shocked at the violence that was abroad in the land. I recall one very prominent executive, responsible for children's programming, who assumed that the violence in children's programming was linked to this social trend. He actually shed tears when discussing it. I, too, believe children and adults are immunized against violence in this nation. In television and other media we teach that violence is an appropriate solution to problem solving. Many adults are quick to resort to violence, fists, knives, guns. Of course, it is hardly a question of media responsibility alone. Parents must intervene to see that violent and tasteless programming does not affect their children. After all, as parents we must pass on our values.

Another strong interest of mine over the years has been to bring developmental child care to as many children as possible. Child care is essential in today's world of working parents, but unfortunately, most child care is custodial child care. As human beings we learn more in the first six years of life than at any stage of human development, and yet we place our kids in purely custodial situations where they grow not one mental inch. For this reason I founded a company to enlist the partnership of business in supplying developmental child care for their employees' children. My founding partner, Lamar Alexander, has worked enthusiastically with me and our staff to demonstrate to employers that developmental child care attracts and retains quality employees, fosters great loyalty, and allows attention to the workplace, all while the child is growing emotionally and intellectually. For the company, the bottom line is in black ink. At this writing, we serve some of America's most famous employers, from California to New Jersey, from Illinois to Texas. Many thousands of children are being developed as they should be and will be great contributors to our future.

My activities in children's television, child advocacy, and child care over the last forty years have brought me into contact with hundreds of people in the media and entertainment fields. Many of these people have made kind comments about "Captain Kangaroo" and shown support for the work that I do, and I'm extremely grateful.

A letter from President
Richard M. Nixon

THE WHITE HOUSE

WASHINGTON

October 13, 1970

Dear Mr. Keeshan:

At a time when television has become such a prominent
part of growing up in America, it is heartening that programs as yours provide such wholesome entertainment.
Captain Kangaroo is a favorite with the nation's children
just as it is with all discriminating parents concerned
with the quality of shows their children watch.

Your special sensitivity toward young minds and ability
to stimulate as well as to amuse have earned you the
deep gratitude of all American parents, and the admiration of your President.

It especially pleased me to note that you are celebrating
your fifteenth anniversary, and I welcome this opportunity
to express the hope that you will enjoy continuing success
in a career that is such a credit to television programming
and such a rewarding influence in the lives of so many
youngsters.

My best to you always.

Sincerely,

Richard Nixon

Mr. Bob Keeshan
20 Melbury Road
Babylon, New York

Harry Reasoner is just
one of the many people
in the media and enter-
tainment fields whom
I have had the good
fortune to know. These
introductions often occur
at a conference or event
focused on aspects of
children's or parenting
issues.

194

```
     THE ASIA FOUNDATION

CBSINC NYK

WU TELTEX NYK D

RELAYING...

U TELTEX NYK D
CBSINC NYK
ZCZC   10268


ZCZC 10005 GOVT NFWASHINGTON DC 89 10-01 953A EDT
PMS MR BOB KEESHAN' DLR
CBS/BROADCAST GROUP
51 WEST 52 ST ROOM 3444
NEW YORK NY 10019
BT

DEAR BOB..
AS THE FATHE OF THREE CHILDREN  WHO WAS NEVER SURE
WHETHERE YOUR OR I WAS THE DOMINANT INFLUENCE IN THEIR
GROWING UP' LET ME BE AMONG THE MILLIONS TO CONGRATULATE
YOU AS YOU CELEBRATE YOUR TWENTY-FIFTH YEAR OF VIDEO GENIUS.
PERHAPS ONE HALF OF THE PEOPLEIN THIS NATION HAVE GROWN UP
WATCHING YOU' AND YOU HAVE BEEN A POWERFUL AND CONSTRUCTIVE
INFLUENCE IN THEIR LIVES. YOU ARE A GREAT AMERICAN INSTITUTION
AND I CAN ONLY HOPE THAT YOU ENJOY ANOTHER TWENTY-FIVE
SPLENDID YEARS.
SINCERELY
   DANIEL PATRICK MOYNIHAN
   U.S. SENATE

1919 EST

1PMTINT NYK
```

One fan of the show has been politician Ed Koch, the colorful mayor of New York, who would always approach me, arms extended, with the joyous words, "Ah, Captain Kangaroo, my very favorite!" Here he presents me with a Certificate of Appreciation from New York City, in honor of twenty-five years on television.

195

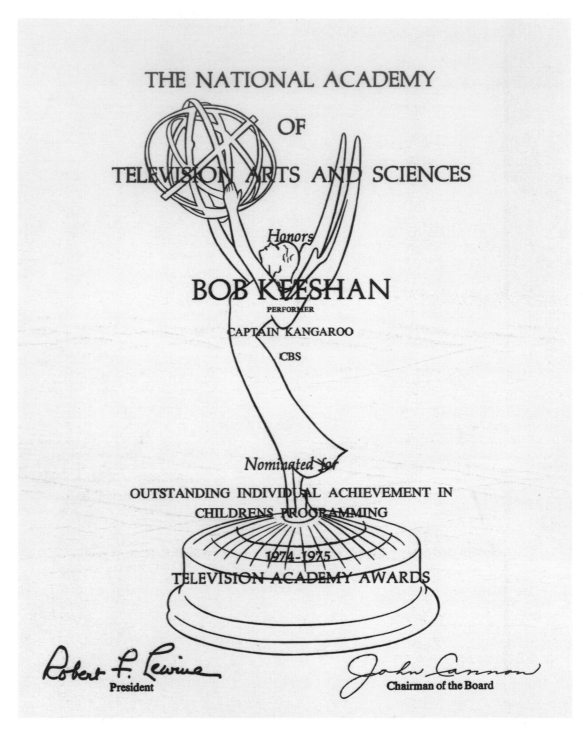

THE NATIONAL ACADEMY

OF

TELEVISION ARTS AND SCIENCES

Honors

BOB KEESHAN

PERFORMER

CAPTAIN KANGAROO

CBS

Nominated for

OUTSTANDING INDIVIDUAL ACHIEVEMENT IN

CHILDRENS PROGRAMMING

1974-1975

TELEVISION ACADEMY AWARDS

Robert P. Lewine
President

John Cannon
Chairman of the Board

Captain Kangaroo" and I have also been fortunate over the years to receive many awards. In addition to six Emmys and three Peabody Awards, I have been honored to have won three Gabriel Awards for radio, two Ohio State Awards, Freedoms Foundation awards, and Television Father of the Year, among others. I don't like to emphasize these accomplishments personally, but I do recognize and appreciate them as an important stepping stone to increasing awareness of some very important issues.

With the gracious help of television personality Monty Hall, I unveiled my star on Hollywood Boulevard. I was pleased and honored to join so many show business legends.

It was with great pride and loyalty that I received an honorary doctor of fine arts in 1975 from my alma mater, Fordham University, in New York.

Perhaps the honors most personally gratifying to me have been the sixteen honorary doctorates conferred by wonderful institutions such as Dartmouth College, where the Keeshan family received four degrees at one commencement: my daughter Laurie, a bachelor's; my son Michael and daughter-in-law Lynn, master's; and I a doctorate. Among other institutions were Bucknell University; Indiana State; Marquette University; University of Maryland; my wife's alma mater, the College of New Rochelle; and my own alma mater, Fordham University.

Through the years of my career and on all the paths it has taken me, I have never forgotten that my work is, truly, all about children. Children are not, for me, merely an interesting audience. They are my life, and every facet of their lives is of interest to me. May it always be so.

A rare photograph taken of the real me. Although I still represent the work that I did all those years as Captain Kangaroo, most of my work now, including the books I write and the speeches I give, are as myself, Bob Keeshan.

Looking Back, Looking Forward

What can be added to a life so rich, a life so full? The answer is, of course, plenty. My passion for the American family and children is greater than ever, as are the needs of families and children. I hope to match my passion to those needs and bring about pleasing results.

I am a multimedia person. I am known best for my work with children, but television has been and will continue to be only a portion of that work. I also enjoy reaching new and different audiences through radio and writing, particularly through books that help improve the parenting skills of adults and the nurturing of children. I plan to work in motion pictures, as I have in the past, when the appropriate opportunities present themselves. I shall continue to speak before audiences interested in solving our many family challenges. I hope always to be a sought-after speaker because it enables me to reach many good people. I also look forward to working in the "new technologies"—the internet, CD ROM, and especially in the many opportunities created by the deregulation of communication companies. All these media will allow me to continue my work for the interests of children and families.

My three children—Michael, Laurie, and Maeve—and my six wonderful grandchildren continue to be a high priority in my life. Like any proud grandparent, I could go on and on with stories about each of my grandchildren. I treasure each child's distinct personality, imagination, and interests. I now get to participate in show-and-tells, graduations, and Parent's Days on the grandparent level, and I truly enjoy it.

I have been privileged to accomplish what we chronicle in this book. When asked of what I am the most proud, however, I answer without hesitation that I am most proud, in this rich life, of those children and grandchildren. For them I will always be grateful to my wife, Jeanne, who knew what a mother should and must be to children. She was a great woman. I count myself a very fortunate human being.

Jeanne and I posed with our grown-up children and all six grandchildren at our home in Vermont in 1991. Our children are, left to right: Michael Derek, Maeve Jeanne, and Laurie Margaret. Our grandchildren are: top row, left to right, Connor McNary and Alex; bottom row, left to right, Kaelan, Britton, Derek, and Connor Matthew.

In 1981, I suffered a coronary in the Toronto airport while on my way to give a keynote speech at a meeting of Parents Without Partners. The Canadian people took wonderful care of me and even presented me with this bouquet of carrots when I left the hospital. A month later I was on an Illinois stage doing a tap dance. You might say I have a positive attitude!

It's a joy that I continue to be invited to take part in fun family events across the country. In June 1996, the Chicago Cubs asked me to throw out the first pitch for their Father's Day game. It was also Family Day at Wrigley Field, and I was impressed by the number of parents with young children enjoying the game and the sunshine.

1. We awakened this fellow each morning and he rewarded us with a nifty poem. Who was he?

2. The Captain often picked up the telephone to make a call but had to go through the operator. What was the operator's name?

3. Out on the edge of town lived a friend in a circus wagon. What was his name?

4. One of our favorite stories was the classic *Mike Mulligan and His Steam Shovel.* What was the steam shovel's name?

5. One of the Captain's best friends lived in a cave and was quite a terpsichorean. Who was he?

6. What was the name of Mr. Bainter the Painter's helper?

7. Who was the invertebrate who often graced us with an operatic aria sung in the shower?

8. Who was the shaggy dog who lived in the Treasure House?

9. What was the name of the blue, dancing hippo who lived with the Captain?

10. Who was named after a fruit and often said, "Da-da da-da dah, ooh!"?

11. In almost everyone's favorite song, a little girl goes to the zoo with her father to visit what special animal?

12. Can you sing or hum the original theme song for "Captain Kangaroo"? What was the title of the British song about a steam engine from which the theme song was taken?

13. The doors to Captain Kangaroo's Treasure House opened for the first time on October 3 of what year?

14. How many years was the show on CBS? On public television? How many episodes were taped?

15. Tom Terrific had a dog who helped solve many mysteries, although often in an unintentional and bumbling way. What was the dog's name?

16. Captain Kangaroo got his name from what piece of clothing?

17. What Mister Moose trick started with a poem, a knock-knock joke, or a riddle?

18. Over and over again, the Captain told his audience about two little magic phrases. What were they?

19. What major league baseball pitcher was nicknamed after a character on "Captain Kangaroo"?

20. Almost every day, Mr. Green Jeans showed and shared information about what?

21. In the sixties, the Captain left the Treasure House. What was the new place known as?

22. Where did "Captain Kangaroo" go when it left CBS television?

23. "Captain Kangaroo" was last seen on television in August of what year?

24. Dolly Parton and other guests saw the family who lived behind the bookcase, but the Captain always missed them. Who were they?

25. At the end of a show, what kind of a day did the Captain remind everyone it was?

26. According to an often-played song, what are busy hands?

27. Who appeared on many Saturdays with lovely dances?

28. Who was the math teacher?

29. A favorite book read on the show made way for what?

30. Although a baby, this orangutan grew up in the Treasure House and even celebrated his first birthday on the air. What was his name?

31. What was Mr. Toot's role at the newspaper? What was the newspaper's motto?

32. What often-read book suggested an odd recipe for soup?

33. What color were Mr. Green Jeans's jeans?

34. What chugged around, whistled, and sometimes carried a bowl of cereal?

35. Just about every day, sometimes even twice a day, a spectacled character pulled a trick on the Captain. Who was he and what was the trick?

36. What drew wonderful pictures to the sound of music?

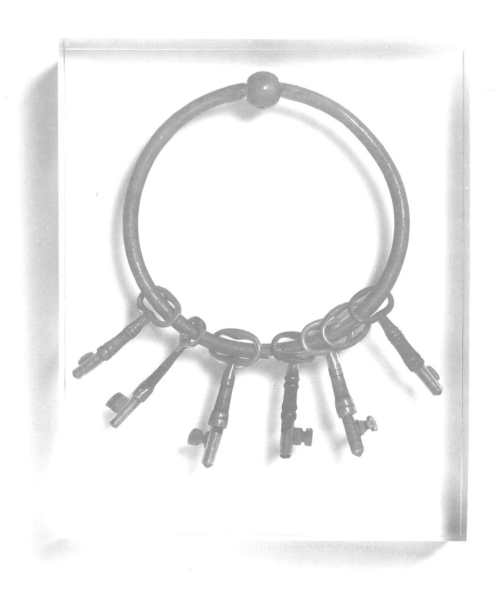

Answers

1. Grandfather Clock

2. Miss Worm

3. The Town Clown

4. Mary Ann

5. Dancing Bear

6. Dennis the Apprentice

7. Miss Worm

8. Beebee

9. Rollo the Hippotamos

10. The Banana Man

11. "The Horse in Striped Pajamas"

12. "Puffin' Billy"

13. 1955

14. Thirty years on CBS; six years on public television; more than 9,500 episodes taped

15. Mighty Manfred the Wonder Dog

16. A jacket with very large pockets

17. Dropping ping-pong balls

18. "Please" and "Thank you"

19. Tom Seaver, nicknamed Tom Terrific

20. Animals

21. The Captain's Place

22. Public television

23. 1993

24. The Little Family

25. "It's another be good to mother day."

26. Happy hands

27. The Treasure House Ballerina

28. Mr. Baxter

29. Ducklings

30. Bobo

31. Editor; "All the news that's fit to print and fresh fish."

32. *Stone Soup*

33. Green!

34. The Treasure House Train

35. Bunny Rabbit tricked the Captain into giving him carrots.

36. The Magic Drawing Board